# BEST PRACTICE

For a complete list of Global Management titles, visit our website at www.goglobalmgt.com or email us at infoGME@aol.com

# BEST PRACTICE

## A practical primer for every manager to implement Best Practice models

*Richard Ilsley*

Copyright © Richard Ilsley 2004, 2010

First Published in 2004 by Management Books 2000 Ltd

Published in 2010 by Global Management Enterprises, LLC.
Massachusetts, USA

ISBN  978-1-61110-002-0

*It's not what you do, it's the way that you do it*
*and that's what gets results.*

## About the author

Richard J. Ilsley is recognized as a leader in the development and implementation of Best Practice models. He has led projects with many of the Fortune 500 corporations and a number of not-for-profit organizations around the world.

He is an accomplished writer having been published in numerous general and industry publications and he is a frequent contributor to conferences around the world.

Richard's organization has offices in the US, Europe and Latin America and he divides his professional time between client projects, speaking, writing, and advising business-based charities, including the Prince's Trust in the UK.

# PREFACE

If you ask any manager in any organization at any level to name the department's top performers, he or she will be able to do it right away. The same thing tends to apply to entire organizations. Ask a manager to name the best suppliers to the company, the best restaurant in town or the best computer brand and that manager is likely to be able to answer immediately. At any moment, some organizations are seen consistently to outperform others, at least for a period of time.

Why is that? What makes these top performers so recognizable and so effective? Why can't we get everyone or every organization to operate at these levels all of the time?

Most recently, everyone seems to have been talking about **Best Practice**, but what exactly do they mean? Frequently, organizations claim to have implemented a "best practice" system. But can they all be "best"? Is there one standard view, one standard approach to each situation or method that we can all use?

So if you have:

- ever noticed that some of the people in your organization seem to perform at a higher level than others some of the time
- ever wondered why some departments or organizations consistently outperform others
- thought that you could learn from the people in your own organization or from other organizations
- wanted to get everyone in your department or organization operating to the same level as the top performers
- ever heard the term Best Practice and wondered what it is all about and whether you could benefit
- wanted to implement a Best Practice model into your organization but were not too sure where to start ...

**... then, this is the book for you!**

# Contents

# Part One –
# The Essential Theory

# 1

# A Brief Introduction to Best Practice

## Best Practice – what is it all about?

The term "Best Practice" is rapidly becoming a cliché.

- Everyone is talking about it, everyone seems to want it and many claim that they already have it.

- Governments, both local and national, talk about efficiency gains available, senior managers in large corporations present it as the new panacea.

- Conferences are held, consultants offer their services and magazine articles are written.

- Cynics say that this is simply the latest management craze destined to go the same way as Management by Objectives, Total Quality Management, Business Process Re-engineering and any other of the multitude of management techniques rapidly embraced and just as rapidly dropped in favor of the next big idea.

- Total cynics claim that all of these concepts are dreamed up by an unholy alliance of management consultants and business school academics to justify their own existence.

- Is the concept of Best Practice just the latest in a line of ephemeral management techniques or does it offer more that that?

- We hear the term "Best Practice" used daily but what is it really and how do we get it, assuming of course that we do want it!

I believe that the ideas enshrined within Best Practice offer great benefits to the management team of every organization—traditional, not-for-profit and governmental—not because they represent the latest business school theory but because they are thoroughly grounded in common sense. In fact, I doubt whether anything in this book will be completely new to the reader. There are no clever processes or tools being introduced.

In fact, the concept of improvement through the application of Best Practice has been used for centuries in different ways.

So we are not looking for brand new techniques to be learned on a two-day seminar, no three-letter abbreviations. The implementation of Best Practice looks at what seems to work best for your organization right now and applying it. Now that does sound simple enough, but as I'll explain shortly, the are a few critical points to understand.

This book has been written for the professional manager, working in the traditional or the not-for-profit sectors, with five objectives in mind:

to give the manager a sound understanding of the fundamental ideas that lie behind Best Practice

to encourage the manager to address the critical (and often difficult) Best Practice questions that will apply to the organization

to explain where Best Practices are likely to be found and how they can be implemented throughout the organization to gain both efficiencies and competitive advantages to provide a ten-step process for the manager to develop and implement a Best Practice process across the organization

to identify the most common reasons for failure in order that they can be avoided.

The book is divided into a series of sections. Each section introduces an aspect of Best Practice. At the end of each section, the manager is invited to take a moment to consider a few fundamental questions before proceeding to the next section.

---

**Having read the book, the manager will:**

feel confident to discuss the main aspects of Best Practice with other colleagues

be able to decide if there are advantages to the organization in initiating a Best Practice development process

understand where to find the current Best Practices

understand the process required to develop and implement a Best Practice process in the organization

recognize the needs and implications for implementation of Best Practice processes throughout the organization.

---

## What do we really mean by Best Practice?

We are going to start by considering one of the fundamental issues, that is, do we all share a common understanding of Best Practice. In other words, do we all know what Best Practice is? Many managers will use the term "Best Practice." Many organization goals state that the organization will demonstrate best practice. Despite the frequent references to best practice, research has shown that few managers can really define in detail what they mean by "Best Practice" and even fewer have any concrete plan to attain it. Despite what some senior managers might want to believe, there is rarely any common understanding beyond the words and the words have started to become a cliché.

The first point that I want to make is that lots of people talk about best practice and lots of people assume that they known what they mean by best practice – but they don't.

I can say this with confidence referring to various research work and surveys that have been conducted.

For example, here are the results from part of a study conducted by my organization. The problem or difficulty of understanding what we really mean by "Best Practice" is seen when we ask managers to appraise their own organizations.

In a recent survey, a range of managers was asked the following simple question:

**"Do you believe that your organization is in the top quartile of best practice performance?"**

Take a moment to consider your own organization. How would you answer this question? Yes or no?

Well, the answer from the sample group of managers was this:

**65% of the managers believed that their own organization would be ranked amongst the top 25%.**

Clearly there is an issue in terms of definition, measurement and objectivity.

So the fundamental issue is that, while many people will talk about

Best Practice, there is confusion about what Best Practice really means. And if we don't really know what it means, then we can't measure it – and it we can't measure it then, as the management maxim goes, we can't manage it. This problem of a lack of clarity and definition of Best Practice is compounded when managers seek to convince themselves that their organization must be "Best Practice" simply because of its size or apparent success. Being the largest company in the sector does not infer Best Practice. Of course, achieving goals consistently through efficient performance is the principal aim of Best Practice but it does not follow that achieving a target is indicative of the existence of a Best Practice process. It could be that the targets are wrong. It could be that external events, beyond the control of the organization, have assisted in the target achievement. There are numerous examples of this situation, including an upward movement of the market, a major competitor experiencing difficulties, a fall in the price of raw materials and so on. Each of these events could have a major positive impact on the organization's business. Similarly, failing to achieve the goals as a result of unforeseen external events does not indicate that an established Best Practice process has necessarily failed.

A more objective measure is to compare the performance of the organization with similar organizations and to look for consistently superior performance over an extended period. For example, we might look for consistent market share growth. Once again, though, we must ensure that we are looking at genuinely better processes and systems rather than the results of a short-term favorable situation. For example, if our R&D department develops a differentiated blockbusting product that achieves dramatic sales, the sales performance should be seen as dependent upon the new product rather than an indication of a Best Practice Sales and Marketing model. Of course it could be that the Sales and Marketing model *is* Best Practice. The point is that, in this example, we should not infer this simply from the sales line.

This situation can be summarized by a comment made by a senior manager at a recent meeting. Asked to comment, as part of a discussion about the opportunities available through Best Practice implementation, the manager replied:

*"We have already done all that. We got all of our managers to implement Best Practice throughout their departments but we didn't get much benefit. What we need is something that is more advanced. We are beyond Best Practice."*

Incidentally, this lack of awareness of what Best Practice really means does not just apply to managing a business. A survey of randomly selected car drivers asked the individual driver to rate his or her own driving skills relative to other people. The drivers were asked to rate their skills. Almost everyone put himself into the top 20%! As in the commercial environment, few of us have any sense of objectivity when it comes to assessing our own performance.

Our first task therefore is to define what we really mean by Best Practice and then to consider the use of Best Practice given the current situation of the organization.

In order to do that we need to get back to the fundamental objective of the organization.

# 2

# Start at the Very Beginning

## What is the organization for?

If you visit your local business library, you will find that there are rows of books written about the role of the commercial organization in the modern society. In recent years, this topic has received a great deal of attention and is subject to a range of concepts and theories. In particular you can expect to find many references made to "stakeholders"; the idea that there are many groups of people who have an interest in the success, performance and behavior of the organization and that sometimes these interests may be conflicting. As a simple example, does the organization exist for the sole benefit of the shareholders or does it have a responsibility to the local community whose livelihood it supports? What do we mean by "organization"? Is it the employees only or does it represent something more? Some commentators have gone on to develop what seem to be complex models to consider the different levels of corporate responsibility.

### The corporate objectives must be the start point

This debate may be interesting and has certainly provided a PhD or two, but we are not going to enter that discussion. To keep life simple and for the purpose of this discussion, my proposal is that we assume that the commercial enterprise **exists for one reason only** and that is **to achieve its stated corporate objective**. In most cases the corporate objective will be the achievement of a level of profit. In the simplest terms, the organization starts off with some money, performs some activities and returns with more money – hopefully!

I am suggesting that we use this simplistic approach because it helps to focus the mind on what Best Practice is all about. It does not matter, from the point of view of the Best Practice model, what the corporate objectives actually are, where they have come from or who benefits. What matters is that there is at least one defined objective. For the purpose of our discussion, I have used profit as the sole objective since it is the most readily understood and accepted objective and because, without profit, none of the "stakeholders" can be satisfied in the long term anyway. Without profit, there will be no investors or money to invest in the business. Eventually, there will be no organization and so no jobs, no community support and so on.

This corporate or organizational objective can be measured in various forms. For example, we might select market share growth as the ultimate measure of success or perhaps some derivative of earnings growth.

So the point here is that the corporate objective itself is not important; *having* an objective is important. From the point of view of Best Practice, ensuring that the corporate objective is clearly understood and accepted is critical, since all of our activity will be driven by this objective.

People are sometimes surprised to learn that I do not regard the corporate objective as being important. If we get this wrong, they will argue, we may put the whole organization at risk. They are right but what they are discussing is business strategy and what I am discussing here is developing a Best Practice process. The Best Practice process is the one that will give you the best opportunity to achieve your objective. It does not tell you if you have selected the right objective. The Best Practice process is certainly driven by the objective.

At the end of the book, I will discuss some of the reasons why initiatives of this nature fail. One of the reasons that I will discuss is the lack of a clear organizational objective that is well understood by everyone. When you think about it, this makes sense. If the Best Practice process is designed to offer the best chance to achieve your stated objective and if you lack clarity or conflicting objectives, then you will never be able to produce an effective Best Practice process. When in doubt – go back to the Objective.

What if you are considering developing a Best Practice process for just a part of the organization? The same rule applies – you must have a clear overall objective. It may not be profit now; it may relate to volume, efficiencies of some sort, customer satisfaction, productivity or cost reduction. The specific objective you select will still be critical for the organization and you will need to get it right. The Best Practice process that you develop will be determined by the objective you select. Once again, if you change the objective, you may well change the Best Practice process.

### Not-for-profit organizations

So far, I have mainly talked about commercial organizations that will aim to produce a profit. I want to point out at this early stage in our discussion that the Best Practice approach works equally well for not-for-profit organizations. We have used the commercial organization as our model for simplicity. If you belong to a not-for-profit organization, then you can substitute a more applicable objective.

By way of illustration, I have worked with (a) an orchestra whose objective was to break even by selling a defined number of tickets for the season; (b) a school that wanted to ensure each student achieved a minimum education standard; and (c) a hospital that wanted to reduce patient waiting time by 20%. You may disagree with these objectives but that is not the point. The point is that the organization does have an objective because it is this objective that will drive the Best Practice process.

## Summary

We have to establish an objective for the organization. This sounds simple and obvious yet countless studies have shown that managers and staff in departments and whole organizations often fail to agree on the fundamental objective for the organization. They will substitute their own informal personal objectives or their parochial departmental objectives in place of the organization's objective and run their department accordingly. The old joke about the store manager who refused to sell any merchandise because he was measured on ensuring that every item was continually in stock may not be far from reality for some organizations.

So you need an objective – and this is the measurement of ultimate success for your organization.

## Achieving success

Having established the objective, the next step is for the management team to organize and plan the organization's activities to achieve the defined objective.

In fact, what happens is that the managers will define, consciously or subconsciously, what must happen to cause Success. Different organizations will use different terminology including Key Performance Indicators (KPI), Critical Success Factors (CSF) and so on. For ease and to maintain consistency, I am going to call these things the **Success Drivers**.

The idea is simple. In order to achieve our objective (Success) these are the things that must happen (Success Drivers) that will cause success to happen – and we should aim to measure these Success Drivers in some way.

### Case example
Let's take a simple example.

We will assume that our commercial objective is to produce a defined level of profit. In order to achieve the commercial objective, the company has to sell a certain amount of product at a certain price to customers. In order to sell the product to the customer, the company must communicate with the customer. Therefore we shall expect to see the company's managers planning a range of customer communication within the overall activity plan. This might involve a level of advertising, having sales people visiting customers on a regular basis or perhaps it may use regular direct mail to solicit orders. There is a wide range of possibilities that will be more or less applicable depending upon the particular circumstances. The more effective our customer communication, the more likely the company is to be successful. Some measure of customer communication therefore will be a Success Driver.

Of course, this is just a simplified academic example to make a point. In reality, life is rather more complicated!

# Management style and Best Practice

I want to pause for a moment to consider management style.

In the same way that much has been written about corporate responsibility and stakeholders, many more opinions have been offered and even more books have been written about management style. A casual glance at the bookshop shelf will confirm that pretty much everyone has a point to make and advice to offer. Many analogies are offered from the military world, although interestingly few if any commercial analogies are used in the military academy! Commercial managers seem to be attracted to the idea of likening themselves to military leaders and frequently co-opt the language of the battlefield, but I have yet to find a military commander studying brand launches prior to an operation.

But we digress because once again we are not going to enter that debate. Instead we are going to consider just two very simple approaches with respect to management style.

## Case examples – management style & Best Practice

Although these two examples may appear very simple, like all the other examples used in this book, they are both based on real case histories.

In our first case, the preferred management style for the organization is summed up by a senior manager as follows:

---

- We hire the best people we can find.
- We set aggressive objectives.
- We offer our people high bonuses if they achieve their objectives.
- Our philosophy is that everyone will figure out the way to be successful pretty quickly or will leave.
- We have no time for inefficiency.
- We are not interested in generic training because we hire experienced motivated people - if they are not motivated by the high bonus and our competitive environment then we don't want them.
- Every year we fire the poorest 10% of performers - that way we send a clear message and continually raise the standard.
- In this organization you either sink or swim - success comes through having an organization of swimmers.

This company is successful and is growing ahead of the market.

Now consider the following approach, once again articulated by a senior manager from a different company:

---

- We hire the best people we can find.
- We set aggressive objectives.
- We offer our people high bonuses if they achieve their objectives.
- Our philosophy is that different people will figure out different ways to be more effective - if we can share these ideas together and offer the learning to everyone, we will be much stronger as a group.
- We are not interested in generic training - we are very interested in sharing the techniques that are currently bringing us most success through specific targeted training and coaching. *cont.*

24

- Every year we develop plans to advance our average performance - that way we send a clear message and continually raise the standard.

- In this organization we all sink or swim together - success comes through having an organization of swimmers.

This company is also successful and is growing ahead of the market.

These two companies and their two approaches are different but not radically different.

There are surface differences of course, but the fundamental difference is that while both companies are currently achieving similar results, the second company is doing so far more efficiently. The second company, unlike the first, is not constantly re-inventing the wheel. In addition, the chances of longer-term success are very much in the favor of the second company.

For the first company, the Best Practice concept is understood by many of the managers, but a comprehensive best practice process for the whole company is not understood or used by everyone. In this organization, each person has arrived at his or her own version of Best Practice, which, as we will see, is likely to include just a few pieces of the complete Best Practice Model for that organization at any one time.

The second company is benefiting from everybody understanding and using a complete and comprehensive Best Practice Model. The second company shares the best proven ideas throughout the company in a formal way. The second company is further benefiting from a culture that continually seeks to develop the Best Practice approach in line with the changing market.

When we look at some of the measures of commercial effectiveness beyond the headline profit objective, we find that the second company consistently outperforms the first company.

## Benefits of the second approach

Our more detailed study of the commercial effectiveness measures showed that the second company has:

- higher profitability per customer
- higher profit per employee
- fewer forms, less paperwork and less management time devoted to paperwork
- fewer requests for ad hoc information
- fewer internal meetings
- greater contribution per product
- higher average production throughout
- lower stock holding.

In fact, when we apply measures based on the organization's ability to add value through the use of shareholders' funds and capital, we find that the second company far outperforms the first.

In reality, neither of these companies exist. They each represent an amalgam of various companies that we have studied and I'm using them to illustrate a key point.

Although the two companies do not exist in quite the neat terms that I have expressed in the example, variations of these companies certainly do exist and we find them in our work almost every day.

My point is that Best Practice is much more than a nice thing to do. Over and over again we find that the organization that implements genuine Best Practice processes (as opposed to paying internal lip service) is many times more likely to outperform similar organizations across a range of efficiency measures.

When I present these two examples, most people accept that the second company's approach is preferable and likely to be more efficient, yet in studies we find that the approach used by the first company is much more common.

## The danger of lip service

While we are on the subject, it is worth emphasizing again that there is a marked difference between genuine Best Practice processes and the claims made by some senior managers that they have already implemented Best Practice.

If you are in any doubt, consider the following questions:

**?** Do you have higher measures of efficiency than comparable organizations?

**?** Do all of your preferred customers see you as the preferred supplier?

**?** Have you recently changed part of your Best Practice process?

The last question may be surprising, but as we will discover, the Best Practice process needs to change in line with the changing environment and, since the environment in which most of us work is constantly changing, then we should not be too surprised to learn that our Best Practice processes are likely to require revision in line with the speed of market change. An issue that we will consider shortly is the phenomenon noted by a number of commentators, that very few managers are able detect the steady changes in their markets until they have occurred. The paradox is that the closer one is to the situation, the less likely one is to be able to spot change until it is obvious to everyone. So the lesson is, today's Best Practice model may not be tomorrow's.

## If only everyone could be like Jane or John!

The reality is that we all consciously or subconsciously recognize that the transfer of Best Practice is the most sensible way forward.

Consider this: If I were to ask you to name the best individual performers in your department, team or organization, the chances are that you would almost immediately respond with two or three names, maybe more. The chances are also good that if I asked the same question of your colleagues, they too would come up with the same or similar names. I've conducted this simple experiment many times with managers from a wide range of organizations. It seems that most people, most of the time, will agree on who are the "best" individual performers. Even when we do not get universal agreement, we find that the same names will among the top few names, at least.

Why is this? Because most of us, most of the time can recognize the results of Best Practice performance.

How often, have you heard a phrase from a colleague along the lines of:

*"If only everyone could be like Jane,"*

or,

*"If we had ten people like John we would dominate this market."*

It works the same way with teams and departments.

Recently I attended a meeting with a business unit of a well-known corporation to consider why the last product launch had not been as successful for this business unit as other business units in the group, and listened to the CEO exclaim,

*"If the marketing department here had the same attitude as the sales department, then we would have had these new products in the market much sooner, and would never have had this problem."*

## Benchmarking and customer perception

And similarly for organizations: part of the analysis we often recommend involves asking a representative sample of the customers to carry out a benchmarking and perception assessment of the company. In addition to the company and its direct competitors, we will also recommend that a number of different types of supplier are also considered in order to get a good cross-section. We have conducted this form of analysis in many different market sectors in a range of markets around the world, and inevitably the same two or three suppliers will be seen as the "best" suppliers by most of the customers in each industry sector. At the same time we may also find that one lesser known, smaller or newer supplier will score very well in just one or two of the categories that we might be considering.

What we are seeing here is a supplier having a positive impact by changing some aspect of its customer support. Rarely is this change recognized by the competitors for what it is until the smaller or newer competitor has become well established. Typically, we find that the larger, well-established companies will ignore the early signs of the emergence of a new competitor or a different approach to serving customers until the new competitor or approach are well established. By this time of course it is too late. It is not just business managers who fail to see the "obvious" evidence. Later in the book, I will introduce a seminal text called *The Structure of Scientific Revolutions* by Thomas Kuhn. This is an excellent book and one that I believe should be standard reading for all managers. One of the points that Kuhn makes is that leading scientists have conducted experiments and have failed to "see" the results, which did not correspond with their preconceptions or with the particular hypothesis for which they were trying to find evidence.

We also recommend that the company should carry out an exercise to correlate the relative scores given to each supplier with the performance of each supplier. The company will often find very good correlation with performance and customers' perception. In other words, it matters what the customer thinks. This might sound like yet another statement of the obvious yet I am often surprised by the number of suppliers who have little understanding of what their major customers want beyond the product or how they assess their suppliers.

A few managers have challenged the level of importance we place on having a detailed assessment of customer perceptions. Their argument is that what we are really measuring is relative size. In other words, they are suggesting that the largest suppliers, by definition, have the greatest share of business. These can offer the best prices and so command the most business and, also by definition, are the "preferred suppliers." Therefore, goes this argument, the customer is simply justifying his or her purchase decisions by saying that the biggest suppliers must be the best. This of course is a circular argument. The best suppliers will tend to win more business and therefore will tend to grow at the expense of the less effective suppliers. This argument does not explain why we will find smaller or newer suppliers scoring particularly well in a few assessment categories. For many companies, we can learn most about trends and customer needs from these newer entrants.

## The purchase decision often lies "beyond the product"

Another argument holds that the purchase decision is all about the product – the supplier with the best product will always make the sale. Experience shows that this is not the case. If it were, then every customer with similar needs would buy one product. In most of the markets that we see today, the competing products and services are very similar. In some cases it is difficult to differentiate between one supplier and the next or one product and the next. In others, the user really does not care. How many consumers are interested in the manufacturer of the paper cup containing their morning cup of coffee? The purchase decision is likely to be made using parameters that lie "beyond the product." Without a comprehensive understanding of these issues, the company is likely to find itself trying to compete on price alone. This may be regarded as a legitimate strategy by some managers, but by definition there can only be one lowest cost producer.

So what is the point? Well the point is that most of us will be able to recognize the results of Best Practice performance and, consciously or not, most of us understand the benefits of spreading it. That is why so many managers want more people "like Jane or John."

## Objective setting and planning

Let us now return to our discussion about objective setting and planning. We have discussed the importance of having an objective. We accept that most organizations will set the objective and then, to a greater or lesser degree, develop what they hope are well-considered plans. The plans will be in different forms and can be simple or involved but the common factor is that the managers or individuals within the organization will each be working to some sort of a plan.

Then what happens? Let's now take a few moments to consider what actually tends to happen.

## Is everyone implementing the plan?

The answer is yes and no!

If each person has a different view of the plan or even a different plan, then we should not be surprised to find people doing different things. But what happens when similar people each have the same plan? What we tend to find is that similar people may still be implementing the same plan in different ways.

Even when the company has laid out a process and taken the time to train the individuals on its implementation, we often find apparently similar people doing a variety of different things. It just seems to be human nature.

# Compliance varies

Many studies conducted in a variety of different environments have show that an individual's willingness to comply with a process can be dependent upon the individual's perception of the value of the process and of compliance.

When the individual does not understand the rationale for the rules, he or she tends to ignore them. Each of us is likely to substitute our own set of rules that we see as more sensible in the given circumstances.

For example, when we are driving, we may exceed the speed limits without any qualms, because we have concluded that it is safe for us to drive at a faster speed right now in these given circumstances. We interpret the rules and what we believe the rule-makers had in mind when they set the rules.

Even the people who set the rules are prepared to see exceptions. Emergency vehicles regularly breach the speed limit.

Opinion polls tell us that most people believe that mobile phone use should be banned while driving – and now the law says so, too – yet some people continue to use their mobile phones while driving. For many of us, our attitude can be summed up as; "It may make sense for everyone else but it really does not apply to me in this situation." Many of us like to believe that these particular laws are made primarily for other people because other people are less skilled, less intelligent, less experienced and need more guidance than we do.

## We tend to comply when we see the benefit

On the other hand when the individual sees the importance of the rules or when following the rules is part of the culture or the normal procedure that everyone has been taught from the start, then he or she is more likely to follow them. For example, airline pilots work through a written checklist before every flight, even though they may have made many flights before and some of then could recite the list from memory. It is a procedure that is accepted and used. It is seen by everyone as a critical safety procedure. The risks of not using the procedure and forgetting a critical element are too great.

Many business writers have cited the example of the elephant and the elephant trainer. It seems that if the trainer chains the elephant to a post when the elephant is young, the elephant will try to break the chain before realizing that it cannot. After a short time, the elephant accepts that it cannot break the chain. When the elephant is fully grown, breaking the chain would be easy for it to do; yet it does not, apparently because it is accustomed to believe that the chain is unbreakable.

In business, compliance to the procedures is by no means guaranteed. In fact we could argue that lack of compliance is guaranteed.

### Lack of compliance may not be a bad thing!

Curiously enough, this is not always a bad thing, as we shall see when we consider the issue of Best Practice development a little later.

### Adherence to the rules may not bring the desired results!

So the answer to the question posed earlier, *Is everyone implementing the plan?* really is yes and no.

The paradox for the organization may be that implementing the plan or following the rules and achieving the objectives are different things. In other words, we may very well find people within the organization who ignore the rules, follow a different plan and achieve better results. Simply insisting on blind obedience to a defined methodology may not be the organization's best option. It could be that different individuals have found a better way.

Within the organization, we will find lots of people will be doing lots of things. Some of those people are doing things that are more likely to achieve the stated objective. These people may or may not be following the organization's defined procedures. The dilemma for many organizations is that while many managers might see adherence to the procedures as the solution, we have found that the organization's formal procedures and rules themselves may not lead to the achievement of the objective. Further we have found that different individuals or groups, who may not be using the established processes, may in some cases be more likely to achieve the organization's objectives.

On the other hand, I am not presenting an argument to allow everyone to do whatever the individual thinks is right at the time. The point is that, from time to time, individuals will be using more effective approaches and these approaches may not conform to the organization's defined approach.

For many managers, this presents something of a dilemma. Most managers recognize the need to promote individual thought and creativity and many organizations positively encourage (in word at least) so-called empowerment. Empowerment is generally taken to mean that the individual should be encouraged to take the initiative at the local level. At the same time the manager recognizes that we cannot have an effective organization where each individual makes up the rules as he or she goes along. In many organizations this dilemma is never properly resolved.

Of course, the answer to this dilemma is simple. What we want is to ensure that the organization's established procedures are followed and that the established procedures are the ones most likely to lead to success at that time. In other words the procedures represent the best thing to do.

Whenever we find a situation where those individuals who do not follow the established procedures can be shown to be more successful than the average conforming individual, then we have to question the established procedure.

## What is the "best" thing to do?

As we progress through life, each of us builds a set of methods or ways of doing things that we believe will offer the best chance of achieving success in each aspect of our life. We each have our preferred ways of doing things; our own set of beliefs about the "best" way to deal with each situation. Sometimes these ways of dealing with things or methods of working have been developed after careful thought and in other cases they have simply developed and have never been questioned. Some scientists will refer to these beliefs as paradigms.

## Paradigms – the route to success and failure!

A paradigm can be seen as a defined approach or set of rules for handling a given situation. Over time, for some of us, these paradigms or preferred approaches become rigid rules. For some they become part of their personal dogma; inflexible and unchangeable. These old dogs are not able or willing to learn new tricks.

Now the curious thing about paradigms is that they both help and hinder us. It is essential for us to have established ways of doing things that we know will work. When we get up each morning we will each have a routine. The routine will differ by person but is likely to include the same core elements. We will tend to dress the same way depending upon what we are doing. The decision for a worker on a Monday morning who works in a conventional office will be which suit, which shirt, which pair of shoes selected from a relatively narrow range, rather than what to wear.

People get into the habit of wearing certain items that they think are "best" for them; although we may not all agree with them! I see other people wearing items or combinations of clothing that I would not want to be caught dead wearing – and no doubt these same people have the same view about my dress sense. My view of what is "best" may not be your view but nevertheless, having a fixed set of beliefs generally makes me more efficient in the routine of dressing. If I had to consider all of the possible questions concerning getting dressed each morning, I would never leave the house.

So the routine (if not the dress sense) helps us. We are more efficient. We get the task completed automatically. We get into the car and drive. When we learn to drive, we have to consciously think about every detail. When we become experienced drivers, we don't have to think in such detail about what we are doing; it becomes automatic. Many people have experienced driving while at the same time thinking deeply about an important issue and later not being able to recall the journey at all.

But the very routine or the rules – or more properly, the expectations that they bring – can also hinder us.

## Thomas Kuhn and scientific revolutions

The term "paradigm" was first coined by Thomas Kuhn in his ground-breaking book *The Structure of Scientific Revolutions*. Kuhn set out to understand the background to major scientific advances. Counter to the expectations of most people, he found that the significant breakthrough was less likely to come from the established scientific community. Very often the breakthrough came from scientists working on the edge of the establishment or from a chance discovery occurring, often by accident. The advance was most likely to come from people who might have rejected the established beliefs and who were working with a different set of "rules" and expectations from the establishment.

Even more curious was the discovery that observations and potential advances could be suppressed by members of the establishment when those observations did not coincide with their belief systems or paradigms. Kuhn found that scientists could actually ignore data from experiments when that data suggested that their paradigms might be wrong and might have to be changed. The paradigm had become so strong in the mind of the individual that he or she could not see, figuratively or literally, any alternatives even when the evidence for the alternative was right there in front of them.

### The "discovery" of oxygen happened twice!

One of the examples that Kuhn uses is the "discovery" of oxygen. In the eighteenth century, two scientists, Joseph Priestly and Antoine-Laurent Lavoisier, working independently, both observed similar phenomena and both recorded comparable observations. In other words they were both witnessing the same thing. Priestly had very firm paradigms in mind and tried to explain his results purely in terms of the current thinking and rules, refusing to accept any other explanation because he just "knew" what was "right." Lavoisier, on the other hand, was prepared to accept the results in their own right and consequently suspected that the existing scientific paradigms needed to be changed in line with the new knowledge. Both men could be said to have "discovered" oxygen but only one was able to "see" it.

## Our paradigms guide our behavior

So we can see that individuals, organizations and whole communities can have their own established paradigms.

For the individual, the set of paradigms will be influenced primarily by personality, education and, of course, experience. For the organization and community, the paradigms are likely to have developed over many years to simply become part of the "way we do things around here."

For each of us, our behavior and activities are guided by our paradigms either consciously or subconsciously.

So the chances are high that each of us will have a preferred way of operating in any given circumstance. We may be aware of other possibilities but we will lean toward a few that are, as we see it, tried and tested. We feel comfortable with the ways we know.

Many managers assume that individuals in the same organization are likely to have the same or similar sets of paradigms. However, this is not necessarily the case. In some cases, within the management team of the organization, the paradigms can vary dramatically. The same situation could be addressed in completely different ways by different managers with different sets of paradigms.

## Case examples – paradigms

As an illustration, here are examples of a number of paradigms that I have seen over recent years, where very different approaches have been used in all but identical situations.

For example, one manager will apply rigid cost management to the organization believing that:

**"a penny saved is a penny earned."**

Another manager, doing a similar job, will concentrate far more on output—how much has been sold or produced—believing that:

**"you can't cut your way to growth."**

One manager will invest time and effort in supporting the weaker performers to help raise their performance: another manager will have a policy of firing the lowest producing 10% of individuals every year.

One manager will want to control every aspect of his or her department: another manager will want to delegate as much as possible to the different team members and concentrate solely on the strategy and direction.

One manager will work (or at least be in the office) from early in the morning till late at night and will bring work home believing that one must to be completely dedicated to succeed: another manager will work the contractual number of hours believing that balance in life is the key to long-term success.

## Which approach is right?

In each case, the individual will be convinced that his or her approach is the best one in the given circumstances.

And who is to say who is right and who is wrong? What is the "best" approach?

We can produce case studies to demonstrate that almost any approach you can think of has led to success in a particular situation – and probably another case study that suggests that the same approach contributed to failure in another situation.

So not only do the individuals not follow the processes, they may also have completely different beliefs about the best processes for achieving the same ends.

### There may be more than one view about your Best Practice!

So two of the difficulties faced by organizations in developing and implementing Best Practice models is in defining just what they mean by Best Practice and discovering that different managers or groups may have very different views about what Best Practice looks like.

### Your paradigms may not be my paradigms

By now we should recognize that the organization cannot just decide to "do" Best Practice because we may well find that different people within the organization have completely different views. This can come as a surprise to many people. The whole point about an individual's paradigms is that the individual is sure that these paradigms offer the best chance of success. It may not occur to the individual that other people have different paradigms. I might think that Jane or John represents the embodiment of Best Practice for our organization. Someone else might disagree completely.

This concept that my idea of what is "best" may not be shared by everyone else is one of the fundamental issues that we must recognize before we "do" anything.

Let's now consider some of the other issues concerned with the development of a Best Practice process.

## Concentrating on the Success Drivers

Let's assume for a moment that we know what we want to achieve or, if you prefer, we know what success means for us. The next critical thing to understand is what causes success in our organization. What do I mean by this?

An example will help to make the point. I will take a retailing example since we are all familiar with buying our groceries in supermarkets.

### Case example – Success Drivers

We are going to assume that we have a product that we want to sell to the consumer. Our goal is to make profit by selling the product. We believe that the retail environment offers us the best route to market and this means that we want to have our product stocked by the supermarkets.

To keep it really simple, let's assume that success for us is the amount of product we sell; in other words we have an objective to sell a certain defined volume of product.

The question we must ask ourselves is:

**What will cause this success (selling product) to happen?**

Distribution of the product seems like a good start. By distribution, I mean the number of stores that have our product on the shelf for sale. The simple logic goes like this:

**The greater our product's distribution, the more stores are selling the product so the greater the chance of selling the product to the consumer and so achieve our objective.**

If fact you could argue that distribution is by far the most important of our Success Drivers. If the product is not on the shelf, then nothing else that we might be doing will have any impact since it is not possible for the consumer to buy the product anyway.

We should be able to correlate distribution with sales: The more distribution, the greater our sales. It is easy to measure sales since we must know what we are selling and we should have a good estimate of the distribution. So it looks simple. Send the sales team out to get distribution.

Our simple logic suggests that if distribution is a fundamental cause of success – a Success Driver – then we want as much distribution as possible. As long as our distribution is less than 100% we should concentrate our sales effort on raising it because we believe that distribution is fundamental to our success.

The approach that I have just outlined is in fact a very much-simplified version of the one taken by many companies. They select a few obvious Success Drivers and throw their effort into achieving them.

Our simple example deliberately considers only one Success Driver to make the point and, of course, in reality there are other Success Drivers of which we should be aware.

### There is more than one Success Driver

The point I want to make is that identifying the obvious Success Drivers - the number of widgets made per hour, the number of sales calls per day, the cost of an activity is unlikely to be the answer in itself. It is just the start of getting to the answer.

There are a few important issues to consider.

## The Law of Diminishing Returns

We are all familiar with the Law of Diminishing Returns. It tells us that as we put more effort into something, over time we get proportionally less out.

We can plot the effort – return graph like this:
The Law of Diminishing Returns

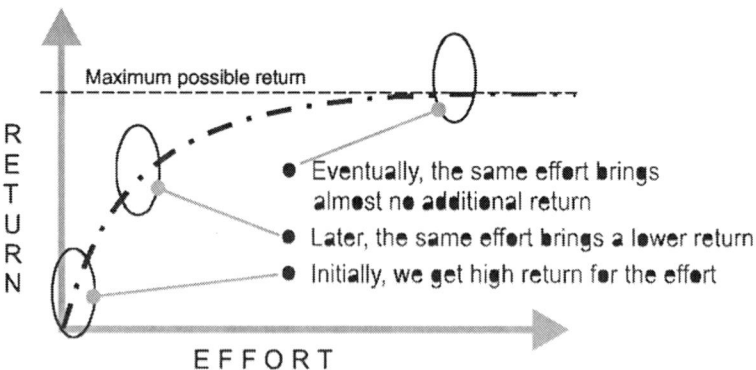

As we progress, the return becomes relatively more "expensive."

In our example that considered selling a consumer product through the supermarkets, we are likely to find that the first few points of distribution are easy to achieve. There are some retailers out there who are willing to take our product straight away. And as soon as we get the product on the shelf, we start to see sales to the consumer.

The next few points of distribution are a little more difficult to achieve because these retailers take a bit more convincing and we might not sell quite as much in relative terms compared to our first few points of distribution gained.

As we go on, we will find that things become increasingly difficult. The last few points of distribution will be very difficult and expensive to achieve and are unlikely to achieve very many more sales to the consumer. Almost every consumer has the chance to buy our product from at least one store already.

## 100% achievement brings inefficiency!

So the question is:

**"At what point in our drive for distribution (the very thing that we believe will bring us success) do we stop trying to get any more distribution because the extra distribution will actually cost us more money than we gain?"**

The answer is clearly not 100%. At 100%, we are very unlikely to have a Best Practice solution since those extra few points of distribution will have been achieved at high cost and will have yielded very little.

The Best Practice solution, or the optimal solution, will usually be less than 100% – ASSUMING THAT PROFIT IS THE GOAL!

If distribution alone were to be the goal, then we would continue to 100% since we would have decided that the cost and profit are not important. Of course, this is not realistic but I want to make the point that the Best Practice solution will always relate to the fundamental objective or measure of success. Change the objective and you change the Success Drivers and consequently the Best Practice solution.

So a key point is that we must be absolutely clear about our objective before we can establish the Success Drivers.

## 80% may the optimal solution

In addition, the Best Practice solution is very unlikely to be 100% of any one of the Success Drivers.

This is a difficult concept for some people to grasp; the idea that perhaps 80% or 90% is the optimal solution. It just doesn't even sound right. But the reality is that the organization has a finite amount of resource and effort available. Not only is trying to squeeze the last bit of return from one area ineffective, it also "steals" resource from another area where a better return could be gained. The trick with establishing a Best Practice system is to balance the effort and return across all of the many Success Drivers.

## Best Practice means optimizing the resources

So the Best Practice solution is, almost by definition, the most effective use of the resources available to reach the determined objective. Rarely does this mean throwing all the effort at one or two "obvious" targets. We need to get behind what seems obvious to understand what really causes success to happen.

A useful analogy is to consider a spoked wheel, as shown on the next page.

Imagine that each spoke represents one of the Success Drivers for the objective of your organization.

Not only do you have to figure out which spokes you need, but you also have to ensure that the spokes are balanced. Too much or too little of one spoke and the wheel will not run smoothly.

# The analogy of the balanced spoked wheel

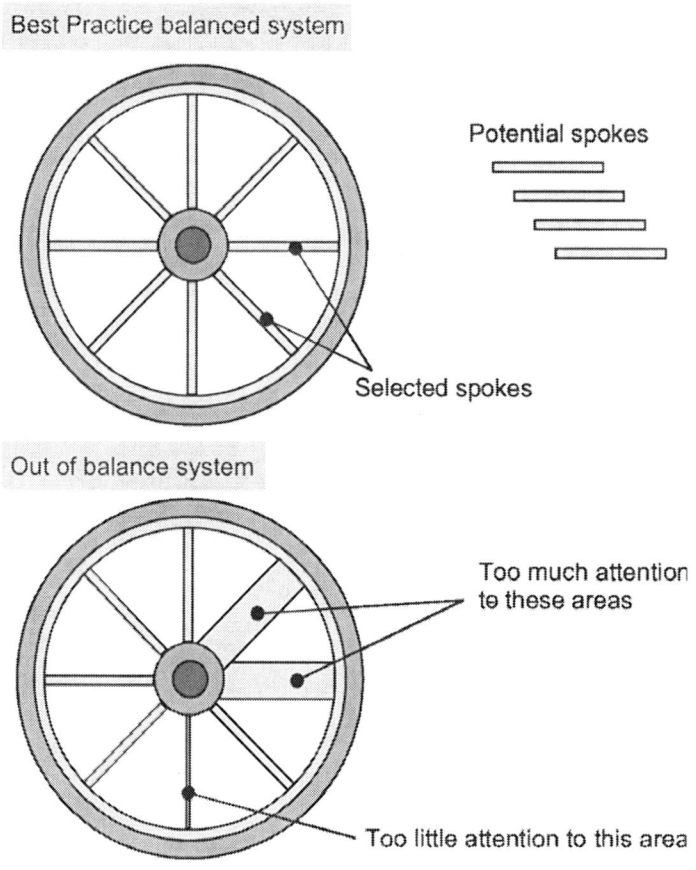

There is another issue to consider.

# Pareto and the 80/20 Rule

In the nineteenth century, an economist called Vilfredo Pareto was studying wealth distribution in Italy. He discovered that the majority of the wealth in the country was controlled by a very few people and that most of the wealth creation could be attributed to a relatively small number of factors.

He went on to argue that there was a universal law of income distribution and of course most managers will be familiar with Pareto's Rule that implies that the majority is accounted for by the minority. This is sometimes called the 80/20 Rule based on the assumption that around 80% of the results are accounted for by around 20% of the effort.

**Only a few of your activities deliver most of your results**
So this means that when we consider all of the activities with which we are involved, only a few of these activities are likely to be responsible for the majority of the results.

When we turn it around it gets a little scarier:

**"A significant number of your activities produce very little return and some of your activities are likely to produce nothing and are probably a net cost to your organization."**

*Case example – hidden losses*
Consider this case study.

A newly appointed senior manager asked for a profit analysis by customer, for the organization. Imagine the manager's surprise to discover that the top 20% of customers were worth 120% of the profits! The manager sent the figures back to the finance department to be corrected. The figures were duly returned with a note to confirm that they were in fact already correct.

The other 80% of the customers actually caused a loss of 20%!

# Pareto graphed, some customers are more equal than others

We can also draw a graph for Pareto's Rule. It looks very similar to the Law of Diminishing Returns.

You can do this for your customers, your team's productivity, your profits and so on.

For example, if you draw a graph for the value of business conducted with the customers, you are very likely to get something that looks like this.

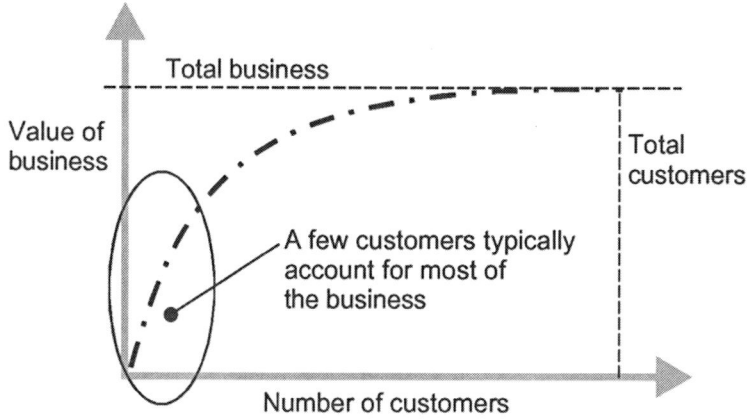

Once again we see that not everything is equal. In our example, losing a customer from the left hand of the scale could have a catastrophic impact on the business, whereas losing a customer from the right hand side might have hardly any impact at all.

By the way, the same argument has been used to propose a reduction of the working week to four days on the grounds that 20% of the week is likely to be wasted time!

## Summary so far

So we know that:

> We need to ensure that everyone understands what we are trying to achieve and how we will measure Success.

✍ We need to ensure that we know what causes Success – the Success Drivers.

✍ We have to recognize that only a minority of what we do or could do will bring Success.

✍ We need to develop a plan that ensures that the right amount of effort is devoted to the right Success Drivers.

✍ Our carefully developed plans are likely to be interpreted in a variety of ways by the people implementing them.

✍ People may bend the rules and substitute their own ideas and this may not always be a bad thing.

✍ Pursuing one Success Driver to its maximum is unlikely to be effective.

✍ Most of what we are doing does not add very much value!

# 3

# Best Practice Fundamentals

## So what is Best Practice?

It's time to consider what Best Practice means.

> **The Best Practice approach is simply the combination of activities that is most likely to cause you to achieve your objectives, in the current circumstances.**

That's it!

This means that the Best Practice approach is likely to involve:

- structure
- processes
- roles and responsibilities
- systems
- tools
- skills.

In fact, pretty much everything that you do.

The Best Practice approach simply says:

**If you do these activities in this way, you have a <u>better chance of achieving your objectives</u> than any other combination of activities, in the current circumstances.**

Of course it does mean that you must ensure that everyone is clear about the objectives! Any Best Practice initiative will be dead before it starts if you have confused objectives.

To make the point, just consider what will happen when one part of the company is focused on profit, another on volume and still another on cost control. You start to see just how chaotic some companies can become.

So the question becomes, what are those things that will make up Best Practice for your organization?

# Developing the Best Practice model

What we are seeking is the combination of elements that together will make up our Best Practice model.

We will expect to see aspects of the model concerned with at least some of those factors listed on the previous page – structure, processes, roles and responsibilities, systems, tools, and skills.

### Sources for the Best Practice model

There are three sources for the Best Practice model;

1. **Within the organization** – in other words you assume that you already have the basis of Best Practice within your organization – the task is to identify it and develop it into a formal model.

   This approach is most applicable when you are confident that you have the basis of Best Practice somewhere in your organization.

2. **Outside the organization** – in other words taking an established Best Practice model from outside the organization and adapting it to suit your own particular unique organization's circumstances.

   This approach is most applicable when we recognize that we need to implement Best Practice but do not have the basis of the model internally. This approach also allows you to move more quickly since you do not have to identify all the various individual components of the model internally. On the other hand, you do have to adapt the external model to meet your own circumstances and there is always the danger of rejection from the "not invented here" lobby.

3. **First principles** – in other words developing the model from scratch.

Occasionally you will find yourself in a new situation or perhaps one where the environment has changed radically. In this situation, you are unlikely to find Best Practice either inside or outside your organization since no one has had the chance to react and evolve a new process.

This approach is most applicable when you need to build a brand new model in order to respond to new circumstances or when you are looking for a dramatic competitive advantage based upon a completely new paradigm.

I am going to discuss the stepped process for each of these approaches, but first I want to pause again to consider common misplaced perceptions about creating Best Practice models.

I find it helpful to get these issues out of the way before we go on to consider identifying and building our model.

# Pause for theory – misconceptions about Best Practice

I want to dismiss some of the common but mistaken beliefs that some managers hold when it comes to building and implementing the Best Practice model.

## Misconception 1
### Everyone will be able to operate at the "Best Practice" level.

The most common misconception we face is the assumption that a Best Practice initiative will result in every member of the organization miraculously being able to perform at the highest level.

This is simply not possible. We are not talking about magic here just different ways of doing things.

Yet we do know that in most cases, when a Best Practice approach is taken, overall performance rises.

How is this possible?

## Performance rises due to average improvement

The answer is that the real gain for the organization is not in helping the better people get even better but by improving the average performance by a modest amount. Since by definition the bulk of the people are grouped in the "average" category, by shifting this group's performance even slightly, we can get significant gains.

## Performance graphed

It helps at this point to visualize Best Practice as a graph.

If we plot Performance (using whatever measure you choose) along the *x*-axis and Number of People operating at each level of performance along the *y*-axis, then we will find that we get what the statisticians will describe as a normal distribution. (This is "normal" in the statistical sense.) Some people prefer to call this a bell-shaped curve, for obvious reasons.

Consider first the common format of the normal distribution. We see a symmetrical curve peaking in the center.

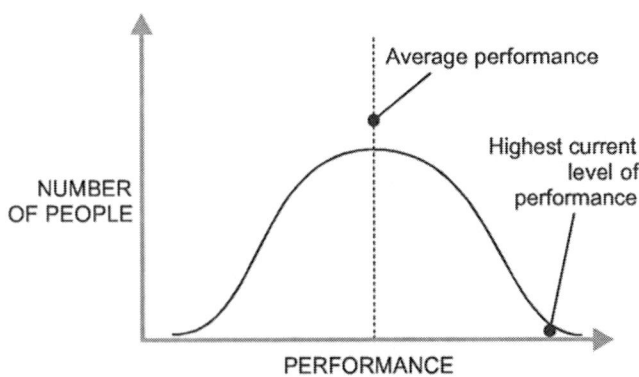

This is the graph that represents the typical "normal" distribution. Naturally, the greatest number of people perform at the "average" level. In this example, there are equal numbers of people who perform above and below the average performance. This is the theoretical result we expect to get when we plot performance.

## Reality is slightly different

In reality we get a slightly different version of this graph. When we plot the real data, we find that the curve is skewed to the right and cuts off more abruptly on the left.

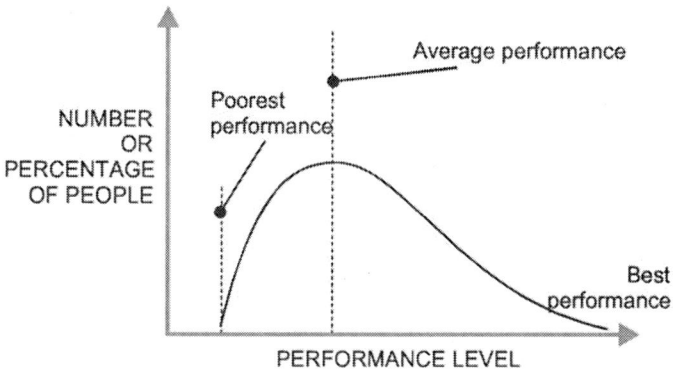

**Typical "real" performance graph**

The curve we plot indicates the number or the percentage of people who are performing at a particular standard. Once again, the average performance is seen at the highest point of the curve.

The top performers are seen on the right hand side.

The poorer performers are to the left.

## Companies are good at recognizing poor performance

Notice that the curve falls more abruptly on the left hand side. This is because companies are, in the main, effective at weeding out the poorer performers over time. We tend not to see anyone below a certain level of performance.

On the other hand the right hand side of the curve continues much further. There is no imposed cut off for the top performers.

If we look at the curve again we can appreciate how best practice initiatives have the potential to have a significant impact. The area under the curve indicates the relative number of people that fall into a particular group.

## Top performers

Area "A" for example contains the very best performers. There are relatively few of them.

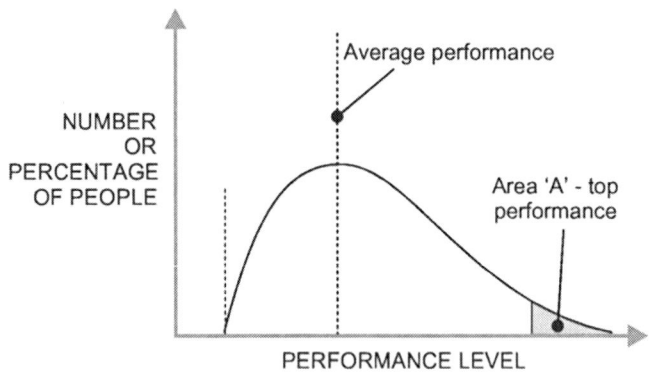

## Above average performers

Area "B" represents those above average performers who fall short of the very best. There are far more of them.

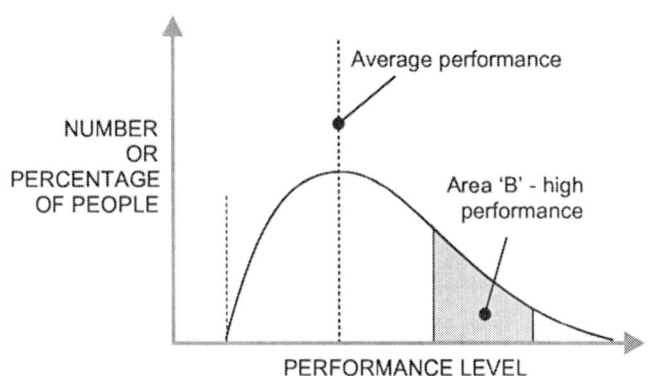

## Average performers

Area "C" represents those people who are grouped around the average performance. This is the majority.

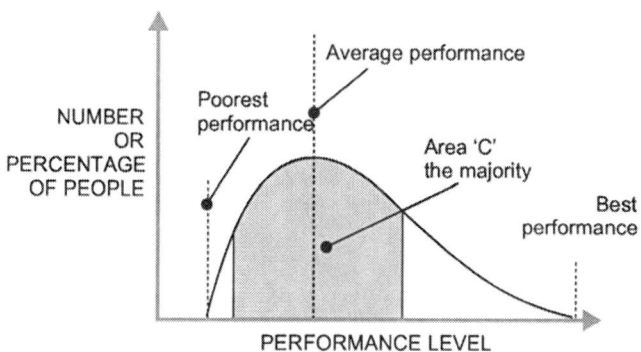

The biggest gain comes from moving the average.

If we could move area "C" to the right, toward better performance, this would offer the most significant gain since it is by far the largest area and number of people.

## Moving the average holds the key to performance increase

This is why the best practice goal is not to help the top performers get even better, or to get everyone operating at the same level as the best performers, since we all know that that is not possible.

The goal is to move the average performance a few points toward better performance.

You can do the arithmetic for your own department or company. A modest increase in average performance can have a significant impact on overall performance.

## The results of the successful Best Practice initiative

Now what happens following the implementation of a successful Best Practice initiative?

Generally what we will find is that the curve has moved to the right (toward better performance). We will often find that the curve changes shape to become more rounded.

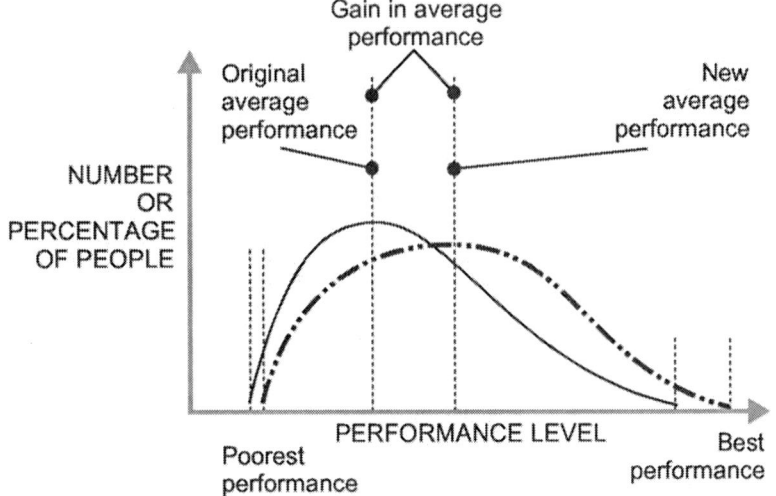

Top performance moves a little also as does the poorest performance measure. But the real gain to the organization is that the average performance has moved substantially.

This is the real benefit of the Best Practice initiative.

A question often raised is "why does the graph show such a relatively small performance increase for the poorer performers?"

First of all, this graph used for illustration is simply one example. It does not represent every case. What we find over a number of cases is that there are variations in the shift of poorer performance ranging from a fairly modest shift, as shown here, to a much more pronounced shift.

It is believed that the reasons for this variation lie with the reason for the poorer performance. In simple terms, there tend to be three reasons why people fail to perform effectively.

● **The individual does not know what to do.** If this is the case then we will see a strong shift in performance because the Best Practice process will define exactly what must be done. Therefore this problem is overcome quickly and the individual is able to perform at a much higher level.

**The individual knows what to do but not how to do it.** Again, this problem tends to be overcome relatively easily since the Best Practice model will explain how to perform the tasks and will provide the individual with the relevant processes, systems, tools and skills to do them. In other words the Best Practice model will provide the individual with the right environment.

**The individual knows what to do, how to do it but does not want to do it.** Clearly this is a very different problem and one which may not be addressed or only addressed in part by a Best Practice process. If this is the reason for poorer performance, then we may find that these individuals are cynical or resentful toward the organization and may reject any initiative out of hand. In most cases, this issue will either be known within the organization from the start or will become apparent early into the process since the Best Practice approach relies on support throughout the organization from the start. Individuals in this frame of mind are far less likely to raise their performance through a Best Practice or any other initiative.

My illustration has used individual performance for ease of discussion but we can apply exactly the same logic and approach to teams of people and to entire business units. For example, we have used the technique to assess the performance of different business units around the world in bringing a similar new product to market. We found that when we had taken out the obvious external differences, the performance of the various business units could be plotted on a normal distribution graph to produce the familiar curve.

We were able to go on to identify the best and poorer performers and so build a Best Practice model for product launch for this particular corporation that encompasses each of the elements that could be seen as common. Of course, when you are considering a wide geographical area, you need to take into account some major geographical and cultural differences. What you can do though is to develop a more general Best Practice approach so that the detail can be applied locally.

## Misconception 2
**Best Practice is vested in a single person, group or company**

Contrary to popular managerial belief, it really is not a question of getting everyone to do what John or Jane is doing. This view demonstrates a very naïve understanding of what Best Practice really is and how it functions.

To understand why it is not a simple issue of getting everyone to mimic one or two people, we have to consider how Best Practice may have evolved in the organization.

### The evolution of Best Practice in your organization

And "evolve" is the operative word. We can think of Best Practice in a similar way to Darwin's theory of evolution. Darwin suggested that organisms mutate by chance and that occasionally these mutations give the organism a better chance of survival. The applicability of the mutation is dependent upon the circumstances at that time. In other words there is no concept of "good" or "bad" mutations. Each is just a change from the current mainstream. The vast majority of mutations are either neutral or make the organism less effective and die out. A very few mutations offer the organism a chance of being more effective than the mainstream and consequently these mutations tend to replicate more quickly given their inherent advantages. After a while, the mutation has become the mainstream. If the circumstances change then the advantage of that mutation may go away. When the mutation offers a better chance of survival, the mutation is replicated and the organism evolves. The mutation becomes the "Best Practice" form. There is no one "best" or ultimate mutation or form. The organism will continue to change so long as the changes offer a better chance of survival in the current circumstances.

### There is no one "best" way

So too with organizations. There is no one "best" form. The holy grail of the "best" management style or "best structure" that so many business academics search for and so many high profile corporate managers claim to have identified is an illusion.

## Today's success could be tomorrow's failure

In 1984, a book was published by two consultants from McKinsey, a strategic consulting firm. The book was entitled *In Search of Excellence* and at the time was widely hailed. The book purported to identify the common factors of success for all corporations. It suggested that there were certain approaches or ways of doing things that all successful or "excellent" companies shared, despite their differences in terms of market place or products and cited 36 companies as "excellent," as illustrations. Within a very few years of publication, many of these supposedly "excellent" corporations subsequently went through very difficult times, failed completely or have under-performed the market. The model for success is not owned by any one person or corporation and today's success does not automatically lead to tomorrow's success.

The difficulty with such panacea types of solutions is that they are simply too trite and so lack real meaning. For example, "staying close to the customer" may make complete sense as an idea but what exactly does it mean for any one organization? There are many entirely different ways of achieving it and some must be more effective than others. Best Practice models must be specific and measurable if they are to have any serious impact. We also have to recognize that as the circumstances changes, the model must change. At some point even IBM has to stop being like IBM, as it found out to its cost.

## The given circumstances are critical

What we see in reality is a variety of different approaches that may be equally effective or ineffective in the given circumstances. Certain styles or structures or approaches work well if all the constituent pieces are in place. They may not work so well if one piece is missing or when the circumstances are different. In a similar way, different management styles are likely to be more or less effective depending upon the given circumstances. The smart manager is the one who adapts the style to fit the circumstance, not the other way around.

I have already made the point that when organizations have conflicting internal objectives, the organization will be ineffective.

Effective organizations, by contrast, tend to be composed of people seeking to achieve similar goals. I have also made the point that different people will use different approaches and techniques, in some cases to achieve the same goal.

Some of these different approaches are the result of the individual thinking through a problem and arriving at a solution that calls for a revised approach.

Others arise through luck or chance.

Still other approaches are brought into the organization by individuals who are used to different ways of doing things.

## Challenging the rules is not all bad

You will recall that we discussed earlier the fact that people change the systems and challenge the rules to suit their own views and perceptions. Now we can see that this is not always a bad thing since it can lead, in some cases, to the discovery of a better way. Not always though, which is why it is so important to have clear objectives and measures. We are not trying to promote anarchy, just a healthy challenge of the way we do things. There is a need for a balance between compliance to the model and seeking to improve the model through changes.

What I find in most of the organizations that we study, is a collection of people and groups, all doing similar jobs in slightly or significantly different ways. Some of these approaches are inevitably more effective than others.

Obviously the better performers are those who are more likely to be using more of the approaches that offer a higher chance of success. That sounds like a statement of the obvious when it is written down yet experience suggests that it is not at all obvious from within the organization.

So the things that will eventually become the initial Best Practice Model are at the moment likely to be spread throughout the organization in various pieces.

## Top performance may not coincide with the official approach

Our current top performers may not represent true or ultimate Best

Practice – they just have found more of the Best Practice techniques than the average performers.

It could even be that our current top performers are far from Best Practice. "Top performance" is after all only a relative term.

It is always worth recalling the old maxim,

**"In the land of the blind, the one-eyed man is king."**

As we have discussed these issues, I have been referring to the initial Best Practice model. This brings us to the next point.

## *Misconception 3*
### *The Best Practice model never changes*

Consider again our definition:

**The Best Practice approach is the combination of activities that is most likely to cause you to achieve your objectives, in the current circumstances.**

### Change the situation – change the model

During the Second World War, the U.S. government used the techniques of mass production originated by Henry Ford to produce huge numbers of tanks, airplanes and military equipment, that the enemy was unable to match. Thirty years later and the U.S. auto industry was forced to "re-import" the techniques of production favored by the Japanese that enabled the Japanese to produce cars more efficiently and more cost effectively than the U.S. plants. Ironically the very techniques that the Japanese used, based on the idea of quality standards, were taught to them by an American, W. Edwards Deming, just after the War, in order to help the Japanese manufacturing industry to recover. It was Deming who made popular the process steps know as P-D-C-A or Plan-Do-Check-Act, which summarizes his logic for process improvement.

When the circumstances change, we need a different model and, in our modern world of high-speed communication and data interchange, the circumstances are changing all the time.

## Change is the only certainty

There are few things that we can be certain about in business or indeed any other environment, but one of them is that things will change.

### "Change is our only certainty."

Markets are in a constant state of flux. Change today is more rapid than change yesterday as new technology, for example, advances our ability to communicate instantly. The speed of change can only increase.

We should expect to see new products and services, new technology offering radically new solutions, new customers, new suppliers, new competitors, new channels of distribution; new everything.

## We hate change

The result of all this change is that the solutions that were the most effective yesterday may not be the most effective solutions for today and certainly will not be for tomorrow.

Intellectually, it makes sense but the reality is that most of us find it difficult to accept. Most of us want to hang on to cherished views, opinions, attitudes and paradigms. We do not want to replace favorite products or change well understood techniques. We accept that change is happening in general but we don't want to accept the particular consequences.

## *Case study – clinging to the past*

One of the world's major pharmaceutical manufacturers was involved in a project to replace one of its top products for which the patent was shortly to expire. This product was significant and had generated considerable profit over the years. Once the patent expires, any manufacturer is allowed to manufacture the product and to sell it under its generic name. The project considered the possible positioning for the newly developed product. As part of this project, a complete review of product and customer (in this case medical professionals) was conducted. It became clear (to me at least!) that the original product must be completely withdrawn by the manufacturer in order that there would be no confusion with the new product, on which the company's future depended. Strangely enough, I found that every time our team wanted to discuss the portfolio of the products, none of the company's senior managers was prepared to develop the discussion. It was only much later that we discovered that the CEO had once been the Product Director for the original product and its success and made his career. He had made it known that there was no way he would be prepared to see "his" product being dropped! It was not until a new CEO arrived some time later that the product range was properly rationalized.

## The story of the frog

There is an often-told story about a frog.

It seems that if you drop a frog into a pan of boiling water the frog, not surprisingly, jumps right out.

But if you take the same frog and drop it into a pan of cold water, and heat the water, the frog will eventually boil. The frog is not able to detect the slow steady change going on, until it is too late. Tough on the frog! Don't try this at home.

The analogy holds for both individuals and whole groups of people. Most of us will prefer to ignore the changes and to stick with the previously tried and tested approaches with which we feel most comfortable, until of course it is too late and change is forced upon us.

How many managers do you know who mimic the frog?

## Best Practice means change!

So our Best Practice model must change. In fact I could argue that the Best Practice approach itself involves changing the Best Practice Model from time to time.

What this means is that our initial model is just that. We do not have to agonize about getting it completely right the first time because there will be many other times. We just have to ensure that the model offers us a better chance of success than the current approach.

As we progress, we will find new and better ways of doing things. This will be especially so because part of our Best Practice Model will include a process to capture and share new successful techniques. In this way our own Best Practice Model will evolve.

## The danger of technology causing rigidity

We have to ensure that we do not fall into the common trap of building today's best practice into such a rigid paradigm that we cannot easily change it. We must ensure that the systems that we may have to support our processes; for example, automated customer management systems are not so rigid as to make change difficult. If you implement anything that cannot be changed easily, then you may well be building competitive disadvantage into your organization. It is a sobering thought for many senior managers that the vast amount of money invested in automating aspects of the organization may never ever pay back. And worse, they may in themselves become a barrier to having effective operations. The solution is rarely vested wholly in the technology. The technology is merely another tool.

## Responding to change may be your only competitive advantage

We need to get into the habit of expecting, welcoming and embracing change.

Welcoming change is not an idea with which many managers feel entirely confident. Yet our ability to react to change may soon become the only competitive advantage we have left.

## Top Ten Best Practice Fundamentals

Over the years, I have studied many organizations that have implemented Best Practice processes, both the successes and the failures. As a result I have been able to summarize the main learning in the form the Best Practice Top Ten Fundamentals. The idea is to summarize and consolidate much of the previous discussion into a set of fundamental guidelines for any organization planning to embark on Best Practice development.

### 1. Best Practice must be defined

If Best Practice is to have any meaning, it cannot be a vague intangible concept. This means that the company needs to be able to define specifically what it means by "Best Practice" so that everyone can understand what the result and process should look like.

In some cases difficult questions need to be asked. Questions that some managers might prefer to ignore. Questions like:

*"What added value does the customer believe we offer beyond the product?"* or are we just another product supplier?

*"What are the activities in which we are currently engaged that add no value?"* or are we assuming that everything we do adds value?

*"What is success and what really causes it to happen?"* – rather than what we would like to think makes it happen.

### 2. Best Practice must be measurable and measured

It is fair to say that if you do not know how to measure Best Practice then you probably do not have it. Applying a measure forces the company to define exactly what is meant and to recognize that performance may not always live up to the definition.

In the same way that some corporations have written Mission Statements that are no more than empty rhetoric, other corporations claim to have Best Practice processes without defining exactly what they mean.

More than just having a measure is having a realistic view of the current situation along with an objective and a plan for development. It is also critical that everyone believes that the objective is achievable.

### 3. Implementing Best Practice does not guarantee a performance increase

Implementing the Best Practice process does not guarantee success – however, it can be shown to increase the *chance* of success.

What tends to happen is that the best practice performers remain as the top performers at about the same level as before. The real gain to the organization is that the average performance rises. If performance is plotted, we tend to get some form of normal distribution. The best practice process will move the average toward better performance.

### 4. There is no single Best Practice person or company

Best Practice is not vested in one person or company. What we find is that different individuals and different companies are more effective at different things. Inevitably individuals and companies have stronger and weaker areas.

We also find that companies are in a state of constant flux. People move on, markets evolve, new companies enter the sector, focus shifts, attitudes change – the net result is that the most successful company of today is statistically unlikely to be the most successful company of tomorrow. This Fundamental Point is closely linked to Fundamental Five.

### 5. Success today does not guarantee success tomorrow

The often-told story about the frog in the boiling water is still applicable. The market is constantly changing. The most vulnerable companies are those whose managers fail to notice the slow changes around them until it is too late. Yesterday's best practice is unlikely to be effective today or tomorrow in the same way that today's best practice must evolve to meet the demands of tomorrow.

## 6. Talking is not the same as doing

Talking about Best Practice is not the same as doing it, just as thinking you have a Best Practice approach in place is very different from knowing you do. This takes us right back to the original question posed at the beginning. Do you believe that your company lies within the top 25% of Best Practice companies? The point is of course that believing is not nearly as important as knowing. Knowing implies that best practice is defined and that we can all recognize it going on around us. Knowing involves having tangible evidence.

## 7. Having is not the same as using

Similarly, having a Best Practice model is very different from using a Best Practice model.

A common problem that is often identified is one of compliance. We often find companies that have invested in revised processes and systems that have been designed with Best Practice in mind yet many people are not using the processes. There is often a strong degree of comfort on the part of some members of the organization to continue with the original approach. In some cases, some of the middle management team did not even regard the new method as being the "best practice" and sometimes they are right. The dilemma that this creates is that the most senior management team cannot understand why increased performance is not in evidence, unaware that the new processes are not being applied in full. Consequently, they tend to dismiss the whole exercise.

## 8. Best practice is not fixed

The Best Practice model is not fixed but will change as circumstances change and as new learning is gained.

This is similar to Fundamental Five but recognizes that Best Practice is a constantly evolving concept within the organization. In other words, it is likely that individuals and groups will discover advances to the current defined Best Practice approach. There needs to be a mechanism in place to recognize these advances and to incorporate them into the overall model.

This idea that we need compliance to the Best Practice process while at the same time challenging it and anticipating it to require change over time is something of a paradox to many managers.

The best way to think about it is to recognize that we need compliance to the defined current process and we need to be considering how the process can be improved. They are concurrent activities.

## 9. Best means Best

If everyone is doing it then it is no longer Best Practice – it is common practice! It is not Best Practice to make products that work that you can deliver on time in the same way that it is not Best Practice to arrive on time. That is just a basic expectation. Once again, having a clear Best Practice model will ensure that Best Practice is defined for everyone and that the definition really does reflect best. Best really does have to mean Best.

## 10. Make it your own

It is a truism that every organization is unique. A Best Practice Model cannot be introduced by copying from someone else's without adapting it to your circumstances. On the other hand, many corporations have accelerated the process significantly by starting with the generic Learning or Best Practice models and adapting it to their specific needs. This ensures that the company does not have to start with a blank piece of paper. It also has the benefit of offering the company a template from which to start.

## Summary

There are many companies that are claiming huge benefits from implementing a Best Practice model. There are others who have derived little benefit. The lessons from both of these types of organizations are:

- ✍  **Make it clear for all**

- ✍  **Measure it**

- ✍  **Keep it simple**

- ✍  **Expect it to change**

# Part Two –
# Putting It Into Practice

## Identifying the Best Practice Process

You will recall that I said that there are three options for developing the Best Practice model; from inside the organization, outside the organization and from first principles. The approach you select will depend upon your current situation and your view of the likely events. In some cases, you may be confident that you have the essence of Best Practice within the organization already and therefore it makes sense to formalize the current approach. In other cases, the best route will be to take an established external model either from one or a number of other organizations for your base and then to adapt this model to your own situation. Alternatively, it could be that there are no effective models with which to start and that your best option is to start from scratch.

We will consider each approach in turn. Let's first look at developing the model by formalizing current practices from within the organization.

# 4

# Developing Best Practice from Within

This is the method that assumes that various people or groups within the organization have already developed most of the Best Practice elements but that it does not exist as a comprehensive formal process. In other words you already have the Best Practice model but it exists in various pieces throughout the organization and these pieces must be formally identified and synthesized to become the recognized model to be implemented. Developing the Best Practice model by identifying and formalizing the various processes and approaches that are currently being used is the preferred starting point for most organizations. Assessing if this approach is viable does require a degree of objectivity that I have already demonstrated is lacking from many organizations. Most managers want to think that they already have Best Practice.

All other things being equal, I generally recommend that this approach is the one to be considered first. Simply moving everyone to the current internal Best Practice position will have a positive impact provided most of the elements currently exist. In practice, we find that the most likely initial solution is composed of say 80% of current processes with 20% developed from scratch or imported to complete the current gaps. We will discuss each of these options later.

The key point here is that although the various elements that will become the formal Best Practice process may currently exist within the organization, they are likely to be dissipated across many different people. Each person may have identified or discovered one piece and be using it in isolation. The organization is unlikely to have collected all of these elements into a defined, accepted model. The task required by this approach is to figure a way to identify each of the individual pieces and to bring them together to form a comprehensive whole.

## To use this approach

To consider this approach, you need to be confident that the Best Practice model components already exist to some extent somewhere within the organization. In particular:

- you believe that you already have Best Practice to some level – you will be looking for something that already exists internally
- you believe that you can identify and synthesize the current Best Practice elements and processes into one comprehensive model
- you believe that by making this model available to everyone, you can gain an organizational advantage of some sort.

## Benefits of this approach

There are a number of significant benefits associated with this approach that we can summarize as follows.

- You will be considering activities that are already in use, to some extent, within the organization.
- These processes are likely already to be uniquely tailored to your situation.
- These internal processes are already proven to be effective for your organization.
- There will be far less risk of objection from within and therefore less risk of failure due to the rejection of "foreign" or "external processes that don't work for us."

## Concerns with this approach

The basic concern with this approach is that, even though there may be some gain in identifying and implementing Best Practice from within, the gain may not be sufficient to warrant the effort and consequently may not offer a sufficient competitive advantage. We can summarize the main concerns.

- You may feel that you do not have the basis of a comprehensive Best Practice model.
- You may feel that there is more to be learned from other organizations.
- It takes time and effort to analyse the internal processes and then develop the model – you must devote resource to this work.
- Your current approach may not offer sufficient competitive advantages to warrant the time and effort required – the benefits may not be sufficient to justify the investment.
- The circumstances may be changing so that your Best Practice is in danger of becoming out of date or may already be out of date.

**Understanding Best Practice from your current operation**
The core idea is that you already have the beginning of an initial Best Practice process within the organization. This "process" is likely to be in the form of many different pieces spread throughout the organization.

The task is to gather up all the different pieces and to assemble them into a comprehensive first draft Best Practice Model.

I have pointed out already that most of us can recognize the results of Best Practice whether we are considering individuals, teams or companies.

And most managers will recognize that the Pareto or 80/20 rule and the Law of Diminishing Returns are likely to apply.

What most people do not know is why the Pareto Rule, for example, is happening. It is one thing to know that around 80% of the business is likely to be derived from 20% of the customers. It is quite another thing to know why these particular customers generate such a high proportion of the business. Similarly, I usually find that most managers accept that a few individuals tend to perform at a higher level. What they may not know is *why* these individuals are the higher performers.

To build a Best Practice model from within, we need to know what is it that these people or groups are doing that causes their success and to what degree these things are replicable throughout the organization. Now, there is a view that claims that performance is all about personality. The view is that some people are just naturally more hard working, more enthusiastic, more intelligent, more "something." The conclusion is that we may be able to figure out why someone is more successful but we will never be able to replicate it. We cannot just tell someone else to be more intuitive or enthusiastic. It just does not make sense, they say.

Certainly personality does play its part. But it is by no means the whole story. We cannot just dismiss Best Practice as the result of personality quirks.

If you are not convinced that Best Practice goes beyond basic personality traits then ask yourself why certain seemingly identical groups of people operating in all but identical environments achieve very different results. For example, different police forces in similar environments achieve very different crime clear-up rates. Schools with a similar pupil intake get consistently different exam pass rates. Different hospitals performing the same operation on patients with the same complaint achieve very different throughput and survival rates. So the point here is that even when groups of similar people are performing similar or identical tasks in similar circumstances, they still achieve very different results. All the enthusiastic, conscientious people cannot all be working for one organization!

Do you recall when you were a child, were you ever told to "do your best."

It sounds fine but what exactly does it mean?

The question is, "What is my 'best' and how do I do it?"

What we have to do is consider what these Best Practice people or groups are doing and extract those aspects that we can replicate. And there will be lots of things that you can replicate.

Although it may be difficult at the start, when managers have adopted this more objective stance, quite often they report that they could see very quickly what was effective in their organization and what was more or less likely to be useful. They found that they were viewing the organization with an outsider's perspective. As a result they were able to differentiate the various activities in the organization on the basis of the value added by the activity.

Another point to bear in mind is that we need to ensure that potential Best Practice components that are identified are really applicable to the whole group and are not just specific to one circumstance. Common sense tells us that not all of the things that the person in the city uses will be helpful to another person in the desert. The model that is the result of our efforts will need to have boundaries to ensure that it truly represents Best Practice. We may find that if we are developing a model for use over a wide scale then the Best Practice components will be amended to suit the local specific circumstance.

So a core consideration when looking at the internal processes and thinking about their applicability throughout the organization is to ask yourself to what extent are these processes applicable and replicable across the wider group.

Now that we have considered the idea of developing the Best Practice model from within the organization in general terms, it is time to consider exactly what must be done.

We will consider the process broken down into its ten core steps.

To illustrate the points as we progress, I have included various examples. All of these examples are taken from real projects, although of course I do not identify the organizations.

## The 10-step approach to developing Best Practice from within the organization

| Step 1 | Define Success |
|--------|----------------|
| Step 2 | Identify top performance |
| Step 3 | Define the Best Practice activity |

| Step 4 | Define the Success Drivers (measures) |
|--------|----------------------------------------|
| Step 5 | Synthesize the Best Practice model |
| Step 6 | Sense check the model |
| Step 7 | Build the detail for the Best Practice model |
| Step 8 | Implement the Best Practice model |
| Step 9 | Measure the results |
| Step 10 | Revise the model in the light of new learning and experience |

## Step 1 – Define success

The first step is in many ways the most important because the rest of the process will be driven by this first step. If we get this step wrong or miss it completely, then it is unlikely that we will derive the benefits that we are expecting. Toward the end of the book, I will discuss why initiatives of this nature tend to fail. One of the common reasons, as we will discover, is a failure to understand what we really want to achieve. This can frequently be seen as a failure to have a clear and well-understood fundamental objective. We need to be clear why this organization, company, group or team exists at all.

### Case study – Why does the organization exist?

A local charity had been established for many years with the aim of providing an environment for members of the community with various physical and mental challenges to live normal lives, as far as possible. The individuals were able to live in managed housing along with able-bodied care givers. There were huge benefits offered by this model including giving people the chance to participate in the community in a "safe" environment rather than being housed in an isolated state-run institution. In addition, one of the aims was that the organization should not rely on state funding. The concept was that individual dignity would be enhanced when the individuals were able to look after themselves. To this end, all members of the organization, whatever physical or mental challenges they may have had, worked together to grow food, work in the workshops and maintain the housing and grounds. Produce and various products were sold through local retail outlets in order to generate income.

The model was very successful and additional groups were established. In order to support the expansion and to ensure a high level of efficiency and professionalism, managers were recruited from commercial organizations. A Chief Financial Officer was appointed to oversee the entire operation from the financial perspective. This individual was highly regarded and the charity regarded it as a great coup that this individual had been attracted. One of the first tasks the new CFO undertook was to consider the efficiencies of the organization, according to the job requirement. The CFO quickly recognized that it would be far more cost effective to sublet some of the land that was used for growing crops to local commercial organizations and to buy in the food that was currently being grown. The CFO recognized that small scale farming could never be more efficient than the large-scale commercial farmers.

When the CFO presented the proposals they were met with open hostility from the original senior managers. A long discussion followed but no agreement was reached and deadlock resulted. A third party mediator was asked to help the decision. The first question posed by the mediator was: "*What is success for this organization?*"

Immediately the source of the problem was revealed. The new managers, led by the new CFO, assumed that cost efficiency was the objective and were developing a set of common measures to be used throughout the group. The original management group believed that providing dignity through self-sufficiency was the objective. The fact that someone else could grow vegetables more efficiently was irrelevant, as they saw it.

The problem of course was that either side started out with a different end point in mind. As a result, they regarded different things as important. But the real problem was that the whole group had never considered and agreed upon the fundamental objective. They had all assumed that their view was everyone's view. The incoming commercial managers simply applied the approach that they had always used in the past; aim to be more efficient than your competitors. The incumbent managers assumed that the self-sufficiency idea was obvious.

This is an illustration of a situation that is all too prevalent throughout business and not-for-profit organizations at every level. Individuals and groups of managers working hard to achieve different things, and each assumes that the objective is obvious to everyone and so no one ever questions it.

So the first step is to define what we want to achieve. In other words:

**What is success?**

or, if you prefer,

**What is the overall objective?**

# The danger of working hard to achieve conflicting objectives

Many people do view this first step as superfluous yet, time and time again, I am surprised how many organizations or departments or groups do not have clarity about what it is they, as a group, want to achieve.

One of the reasons this happens is that each group of people tends to assume that the objective is obvious and consequently does not need to be defined. They assume that everyone else will see things as they do. The reality is generally quite the opposite.

As a consequence, we often find people throughout the organization working hard – to achieve different and even conflicting objectives. Managers are surprised when we discuss this issue with them yet a simple test makes the case time and time again.

We ask the members of the team individually to write down their group's primary objective and secondary objectives. Alternatively, we have the individuals select the objectives from a list of possibilities. Inevitably we are faced with a whole host of conflicting views.

A variation on the theme is to ask a group of individuals, each of whom is doing the same or a similar job, to write down from scratch or select from a list the objectives for their role. Once again, it is a bit like asking a group of economists for an opinion; the result is a list of different and conflicting answers.

The problem is exacerbated when different people or departments are rewarded for different or conflicting objectives.

Consider the following simple example.

## Case example – Conflicting goals

Within a large commercial organization, the each General Manager was measured on the profit generated by his or her Business Unit. The Regional Vice President (responsible for a number of Business Units spread across several countries) was measured on the profit generated by the region, of which the Business Unit is a part. So far so good – two managers in the same reporting line both measured by the same form of objective or complementary objectives.

In order to grow the regional business, the Regional VP saw the opportunity to agree regional deals with major customers. These deals included better trading terms across the whole of the region for a customer in exchange for guaranteed business across the whole region. As a consequence, the company at the regional level increased its overall business. However, the terms agreed by the Regional Manager had to be attractive enough for the customer in order to gain agreement to such an arrangement. This deal undermined previous deals struck with the local customer by the local General Managers by effectively reducing the local terms.

As a consequence, the region made more profit through selling more product (although at a lower margin) but some of the local Business Units made less profit since the Business Unit was selling the same amount of product but now at a reduced price. The Regional VP got the bonus but the local General Manager did not.

The local General Managers had done everything asked of them but the Business Unit had not achieved the objectives because of actions taken by another manager pursuing another similar but conflicting objective. Overall the corporation achieved better commercial results in the short term yet sowed the seeds of dissatisfaction and inefficiency for the medium term.

Here is another example.

## Case example – Controlling spending

The Marketing Manager can prove that the investment in a marketing initiative will realize a gain in market share. The Chief Financial Officer is measured on reducing costs, which of course will include sales and marketing spending. To achieve the financial objectives, the CFO imposes a blanket spending freeze on the entire business. If the CFO achieves his objective, the company will in effect reduce its spending and so increase its profit and the business will not gain the extra share which may have led to increased profits and long-term market development.

Incidentally, this last example represents a common conflict between the need to reduce cost and the need to invest in the business. The problem begins when organizations see cost as an isolated item rather than as an investment that should always have some form of return. My experience is that significant sums of money could be saved (recall the Pareto effect) if organizations took a more aggressive stance toward requiring the demonstration of the return expected from spending, especially in a sales and marketing environment, rather than simply basing their investment plan on matching the competition or repeating last year's plan. The argument of "we spent this amount last year so we should spend rather more this year if we want growth" is no justification.

In reality things can be more complicated than the two examples suggest but the point made remains the same. There has to be a clear fundamental objective, which is then translated into complementary objectives down the line. Everyone has to know what he or she must do and the objectives must be in harmony. If people are unclear or if the system is designed to produce conflict, then problems and inefficiency will invariably result.

Now this may sound like the most basic thing that you have ever heard, yet it's worth pausing for a moment to recognize that time and time again studies show that managers in more than 80% of organizations surveyed admit to having conflicting internal objectives.

Once again, a useful and simple task, and one that I generally recommend at the very start of any initiative, is to ask the individuals from a team or group to write down the primary objective and secondary objectives for the team or the group. The results can be quite sobering.

While we are discussing objectives, it is also worth pointing out that the objective needs to be measurable. An objective without any method of measurement is almost as useless as having no objective at all. If you have no measure then how will you know when the objective has been achieved? Again this will sound basic to many managers yet I have found that some of the largest corporations containing the most highly experienced and paid managers are riddled with groups of people who have only vague notions of what they are striving for and have no sense of measurement. Activities and routine tend to have taken over and everyone assumes that everyone else knows what the group is seeking to achieve. "It's what we always do," is always a good indication of problems as it suggests that the people within the organization stopped thinking and questioning some time ago.

Having no clarity over the measure for the objective is similar to having those vague so-called Mission Statements so popular with some senior managers—lots of words that sound very fine yet have no real meaning and do not lead to any long-term focused activity. We have found that most of these "we will be the best" style Mission Statements not only have little commercial impact but, worse, allow people to become cynical about the organization. How do we know this? Surveys have been conducted among customers to look for correlation between those suppliers that claim to be seeking to be the "best" and the perception of the customer. There is no correlation because "best" has no meaning and does not determine behavior or action. It is just empty rhetoric.

### Case example – What is "best"?

As a final example to make the point, consider this large manufacturing organization. A new CEO had worked hard to ensure that everyone understood that the objective was to be the "best supplier in the category." The CEO was convinced that everyone was clear about the objective, and he was right. It was only when each member of the senior management team was asked how he or she interpreted "best" that the problem was revealed. For some it meant most profitable, for others the biggest in terms of share, one believed that it meant the highest customer service scores while another believed that it referred to the widest range of the most innovative products. Each could have been correct and each objective would lead to different behavior and action.

So the first task is to define the objective and to ensure that everyone accepts it. Then we need to ensure that the objectives that are derived for the groups and individuals do really support the overall objective – that is the more tricky part.

At the same time there is a need to ensure that measurements and rewards are in harmony.

## *Step 1 – Define success*
Ask yourself:

What is success for us?

Am I sure that everyone in the organization defines success in the same way?

Do we have clear measures and rewards?

Am I sure that the measures and rewards we use are in harmony?

# Step 2 – Identify top performance

So far we have identified or confirmed what it is that we want to achieve (the Objective) and we have ensured that everyone agrees that this is indeed the overall measure of success for the organization. We have also reviewed the objectives through the organization to look for possible conflict, although we do not need to be too concerned about conflicting objectives at this stage if we plan to implement a revised Best Practice model because part of the model involves defining the measures. On the other hand, if you are simply conducting an audit then you will certainly want to follow through the objectives at each level.

The next step is to identify where in the organization we are closest to achieving the objective. In other words *where* is Best Practice. For example, we want to know where we experience the highest growth, the greatest level of profit, the highest returns per person, the highest pass rate and so on, depending upon the overall objective.

Once again this might sound obvious. After all, surely everyone knows where the best performance lies. The answer is that sometimes it is obvious and we achieve universal agreement and sometimes it is not and heated debates develop about which business unit or department or individual really achieves the best results. By way of simple illustration, is the best sales person the one with the highest sales? Many people would argue that this is the measure of success. Yet what if one person is in the city and one in the villages? In other words, the environment is not equal. Then gross sales may not be the best measure since the person in the city will always have higher sales.

## Where is the best performance?

We want to consider where in the organization we have the best performance, given that the approach we are currently following is based on the idea that we have Best Practice already within the organization. "Best" performance means the performance that seems to achieve the objective most often and consequently where we expect to find activities that are most likely to bring us the success we need.

When you are considering what "best" might mean, it is important to go beyond bland concepts such as "high quality products," "good service" or "professional managers." These are examples of terms that are frequently used by organizations to explain high performance yet have no real meaning. What, after all, do we mean by "high quality products"? What do you expect people to do if they are told to provide "good service"?

I have talked about the importance of having a clear objective. Quite often, when we are looking for top performance, we will actually be looking for the things that we either know or feel reasonably confidently will deliver this objective.

If we use the objective of profit, the first task is to identify those parts of the organization that are most profitable and then to identify why those parts are most profitable. For example, are the most profitable units the ones that drive down costs ruthlessly or are they the ones that concentrate on delivering the highest customer service or both (or neither) of these things? We want to get an idea of what is producing higher profitability. This in turn will help us to get an understanding of what it is we are looking for.

So, if profit is the objective, then we might be looking for the most profitable customers, the most cost efficient production units, the lowest marketing spend per case and so on. What we are doing here is translating the overall objective into subsidiary allied objectives that we are fairly confident will lead to the achievement of the main objective. If we have highly cost efficient production units, efficient marketing spend and highly profitable customers then we can feel confident that we are likely to have a profitable business.

Once we are clear what we are looking for, most of the time it is quite a simple matter to identify the best performance. We can measure which customers are the most profitable, which sales people are most successful, which lines are most productive, produce the lowest waste and so on. Once we have determined that it is not the sales person with the highest sales but the sales person with the highest growth or the lowest customer churn or the highest average customer volume or profitability, then we can determine where this level of performance exists right now. In other words we can identify

Best Practice, as it exists at the moment.

## Don't worry about the detail at the start

Sometimes we will find that the detail evades us and we will have to make guesses or consider more involved analysis but for the most part we should be able to get at least a good idea where our best performance lies.

It is worth stressing again that we are looking for indications of where our top performance lies. This is rarely a scientific exercise, at least at the start, and we can always revise our opinion and change our minds. My point here is that we can always revise our view later. Endless analysis at the start rarely pays off especially if the conclusion from the exercise is that we want to make significant changes.

## Always question – never assume

At the same time we must be wary of making assumptions. On occasions, we will find that managers will make assumptions relying on received wisdom. In fact, it is not unusual to find that performance that had previously been considered to represent "best" is not in line with the overall objective.

A simple example from a case study should make the point.

## *Case study – customer satisfaction may not be a good thing!*

A manufacturer found that there was a good correlation between the manufacturer's share of the customer's business and customer satisfaction. No great surprise there; the more satisfied the customer was with the manufacturer, the more likely the customer was to give the manufacturer the business. It was also found that there was a strong correlation between a few specific sales people and the highly satisfied customers. Good again – we have a few sales people who seem to be able to deliver a very high level of customer satisfaction and this leads to increasing business.

So the logic of Best Practice says – find out what these sales people are doing and replicate their activities across the whole sales force because this is surely the closest thing to Best Practice right now. Unfortunately in this case, this was not so! The reason was that in this case the fundamental Objective was to raise profit but over time an unofficial assumption had developed that the volume and customer satisfaction were the keys to success.

Further analysis showed that the customers with the highest levels of satisfaction were also the least profitable despite the increasing volume. The reason was that the sales people were spending very heavily on these customers in a variety of ways including spending a great deal of time with them and giving away ever greater discounts. This extra investment eroded the tight margins and resulted in higher volume but lower profits for the manufacturer. No wonder the customers were satisfied!

Since the manufacturer's stated objective was increased profit, we can see that this activity could not be classed as Best Practice as it did not serve to achieve the objective. Now, if this manufacturer could figure out how to preserve the margin while at the same time increase customer satisfaction and volume, then it would have something.

So the note of caution is sounded to ensure that we do know what it is that we really want to achieve and to ensure that what we may consider to be our current Best Practice is indeed Best Practice.

## Summary

At the conclusion of this step, we will have identified where current Best Practice seems to lie by looking at those parts of the organization where we seem to have the highest performance. We will have identified particular groups, individuals, types or segments and so on. The next step is to figure out exactly why we get better performance from these areas.

## *Step 2 – Identify top performance*
Ask yourself:

> Do we know where we are most successful?
>
> _____
>
> _____
>
> _____
>
> _____

> Can we measure it?
>
> _____
>
> _____
>
> _____
>
> _____

> Are we sure that this really is Best Practice?
>
> _____
>
> _____
>
> _____
>
> _____

## Step 3 – Define the Best Practice activity

Now that we have identified the location of Best Practice within the organization, we need to figure out what is causing it to occur.

This is rather trickier that the previous step. Despite the warnings given earlier, it is still relatively straightforward to identify the top performance in the organization.

## Figure out *why*

What is more important though is to understand why and how this performance is happening. It is only by understanding why and how that we can begin to consider the initial Best Practice model.

A common response in seeking to understand what is happening to cause Best Practice is to suggest that we simply ask those individuals or groups deemed to represent Best Practice. This does sound very sensible but strangely enough, experience shows that it does not result in anything like a comprehensive answer.

## We can't just ask the Best Practice performers!

There are a number of reasons for this.

The first reason is based on the "can't see the forest for the trees" paradox. We have all experienced this phenomenon. The closer someone is to a situation, the less objective that person becomes and the more difficult it is for the person to see what might be obvious to the outsider.

The difficulty is that the practitioners do not have an objective view and find it very difficult, if not impossible, to compare what they are doing with what the average person might be doing. Most of the time they really do not know what is happening in comparable areas and so it really is difficult for the practitioner to determine the differences. For example, few people actually have a detailed knowledge of what other people in a similar role are really doing. Few managers will be intimate with the detailed approach and methods of colleagues.

Allied to this situation is the fact that many Best Practice practitioners may not regard themselves, or more specifically the things they may be doing, as unusual. We have found that there is a tendency to assume that those people who are deemed to represent Best Practice assume that they are simply doing the job. There is a tendency for each of us to believe that everyone does what I do and I do what everyone else does.

## You need detail

It is normal to find that the top performers are not able to offer a detailed analysis of what it is that they are doing that causes the difference in performance. At most they tend to offer rather generic reasons such as "I always look after my people," "I try to communicate effectively," "I insist on the best quality," "I just work hard" and so on. None of these is necessarily incorrect but the lack of objective detail makes them all but impossible to replicate. We simply do not know the detail of what actually happens. Telling everyone else to work hard and look after his or her people is unlikely to have much impact or raise performance!

### Managers can rarely explain Best Practice
If the actual practitioner may not be able to help, another response is to ask the line manager why certain individuals, customers, departments, groups and so on are more effective. Again I have found that we do not get a sufficiently detailed or objective answer.

There are a number of reasons.

## *Case example – Best Practice assumptions*

Managers make all sorts of assumptions. In one extraordinary case, I found a senior manager who believed that he had implemented a particular initiative and put the success of his department down to this initiative. The reality was found to be that the operational managers had a very poor relationship with this senior manager. As a group, they had ignored the manager's instructions completely and had developed their own quite different approach. Not surprisingly, they were reluctant to communicate this with the senior manager who remained in total ignorance of what was actually happening in his department.

### Senior managers lack detail
Of course this is an extreme situation to make the point. The point is that it is not unusual for us to find that the senior manager may not have sufficient detailed understanding of what actually happens to make the difference between ordinary performance and Best Practice.

### Managers often leave the top people alone

Even though line managers are generally able to identify the top performers, they may find it difficult to explain the top performers' approach in any detail. There is a management style, which we frequently observe, whereby the line manager will let the top performers get on with the job with little interference or intervention. "John knows what he is doing and does not need any help from me." The line manager tends to spend more time with those members of the team who need more help and support. This is a perfectly natural response but it does mean that the line manager is unlikely to have a detailed knowledge of Best Practice.

### Some managers assume the company knows best

Line managers have a further difficulty. For very good reasons, they want to believe that they fully understand what is happening with their team but at the same time many will have an inbuilt sub-conscious bias. Not only will they tend to assume that their instructions are being implemented entirely, they will also tend to assume that the company-defined way is the best way. This is a reasonable assumption. After all, the manager is paid to implement the company policies.

### Getting visibility for the better approach

The dilemma occurs when, from time to time, we find that an individual or team will have developed, by accident or design, a different approach that may offer more chance of success. The manager may not see it and the individual may not want to volunteer it, particularly if it is clearly in defiance of company policy.

Each of us wants to think that our way is the best way. Each of us would like to think that our approach is more effective than our colleagues. This is especially true in organizations with departments that unofficially compete with each other.

We have found that managers may be inclined to put forward their own activities or their team's activities as Best Practice whether they are or not. The natural desire is to want to promote one's own ideas or one's close colleagues' ideas over a perceived rival.

## The problem of "NIH" – not invented here

The counter view also tends to hold. Something that has been invented by one department may be viewed with suspicion if not downright hostility by another department. Consider trying to persuade the French General Manager that the British General Manager has discovered a better approach or vice versa and you get the idea. You can insert your own departments in place of the French and British!

So, paradoxically, those people closest to the action may be the least likely to be able to provide an objective and comprehensive assessment.

## We can test the model with the practitioners

However, we find that, later in the process, it is perfectly reasonable to check or test the derived Best Practice Model with the practitioners, as we will discuss shortly. Although the top performer may not be able to articulate the differences between his or her activities and the average performer, the top performer will be able to comment on the accuracy and viability of the derived model when it is laid out.

## Best practice is not one person

There is another issue that we need to understand. A fundamental concept, that is not always fully recognized, is that Best Practice is rarely embodied in one person or one team or one anything.

What we normally find is that elements of what will ultimately become the Best Practice model are likely to be distributed across a number of people and groups.

Different people will have found different activities that seem to be more effective. These different activities will have been discovered by luck, accident and design or may have been brought in from another environment.

As a consequence, in most cases it is unlikely that any single person or team represents what will be developed as the Best Practice model. The caveat here is that we may find at least much better practice vested in one group following a merger or acquisition. We will return to this area later when we talk about developing a Best Practice model by bringing in learning from outside the organization.

## The benefits of disinterest

By now you will have got the idea that you need to use people who are not intimately connected with the Best Practice activities in order to discover the Best Practice elements. Whether you use people from inside or outside your organization is less important. What is most important is that these people arrive with no preconceived views and are prepared to ask the naïve questions.

## The detective approach

To make the whole idea come alive, I like to think that the ideal approach is embodied by the fictional American TV detective "Columbo" played by Peter Falk. This is a rather dated show now but nevertheless still enjoys a following. In the show, Peter Falk's character, who will of course be investigating a murder, adopts an apparently naïve approach, makes no assumptions and tests every theory to its limit. He is non-threatening in terms of style and appearance. All the time he will be using a series of logical questions and will never be afraid to ask the one question that no-one else would feel comfortable asking. He is also constantly sharing his doubts with almost anyone who will listen in order to test the ideas. I also use "Columbo" as an example to demonstrate effective questioning. If you have seen the show, you will recall that the most important question is always left to last and added as an apparently simple coda that just happened to come to mind.

## Ignorance ensures the basic questions get asked

I know this may seem strange to many people but generally speaking I find that someone who is not well acquainted with the job is better at understanding the difference between average performance and Best Practice performance than someone who is doing the job every day and who consequently will make all sorts of assumptions. Inevitably, this person will be communicating frequently with the practitioners but, like Peter Falk's "Columbo," will aim to keep an objective distance and to question everything.

## Best is only relative

Of course, in order to analyze Best Practice, we will need to use a benchmark point of reference. We tend to use the perception of "average" performance as the benchmark since this helps to define the Best Practice activity more easily. If you know what the average person does, then you will find it much easier to identify what the top performer does that makes all the difference.

So the approach is to define the current Best Practice by comparing the activities of the top performers or those areas that yield the best results with the equivalent activities of the average performers or results.

The way to do this is by having a number of people who are not intimately acquainted with the processes "map" the activities of the top performers and the average performers. What they are looking for are the differences between the two. If the "map" is accurate then the differences should be clear.

We must also bear in mind that "best" is only a relative term. What is best right now will not always be best. I will discuss this idea of continual development through continual questioning later.

For now you just need to have a good sense of what the current "best" performers are actually doing.

## Representation of Best Practice

A frequently asked question is: *"How should we represent Best Practice?"*

I have found that the most effective approach is to use flow chart "maps." The flow chart simply defines the sequence of activities for each area that are seen as Best Practice. The benefit of this approach is that it forces everyone to concentrate on what is really happening. This helps to eliminate vagueness. It also allows us to see the difference between different individuals and groups far more easily since their respective activities are laid out.

Along with the processes, we should note the tools and skills that are being employed. Again this will help to define exactly what current Best Practice looks like.

At this stage we are likely to find that we have a number of versions of Best Practice because different top performers and groups will use different approaches. Not everyone does the same thing. This is fine because later we will synthesize these different aspects into one combined model.

Before we do that we need to figure out the "causes" of Best Practice.

## *Step 3 – Define the Best Practice activity*
Ask yourself:

What is the most effective way for us to determine our current Best Practice activities?

_____

_____

_____

Do we know what it is that causes the higher levels of performance?

_____

_____

_____

Are we sure that we have identified all of the elements that are likely to be spread throughout the organization?

_____

_____

_____

# Step 4 – Define the Success Drivers

So far, we have identified or confirmed and gained agreement on what it is that we want to achieve (the Objective) and we have identified, so far as we are able, those activities that seem to represent Best Practice.

The next critical step is to confirm those things that cause Best Practice to occur. I am going to call these things the Success Drivers. We will come to recognize that there will be a range of Success Drivers and different ones are likely to be more or less important at different times. We will also recognize that the Success Drivers may not have a constant, uniform impact on the objective or the business and we will probably want to revisit our list of Success Drivers in order to amend and add to it at a later date. Finally we will recognize that the steps I have already outlined may be combined into a series of iterations that will lead to defined Best Practice. The actual process may not be quite so linear as I have so far suggested.

It is by considering where we seem to be closest to achieving the objective, that we will be able to go on to consider what actually causes success. These causes of success are termed the Success Drivers and their identification lies at the heart of an effective Best Practice model.

For example:

- If we think that "customer satisfaction" is a Driver, then we would want to determine which customers are the most satisfied and what we mean by "satisfied."

- If "customer profitability" is a Driver, then which customers generate the most profit and why?

- If "product innovation" is a Driver, then where have we been most innovative and how do we measure "innovation"?

- If "market share" is a Driver, then which sales people, which marketing activities, customers and sectors demonstrate the best share growth?

… and so on.

At the same time, we can double check to ensure that our Success Driver choice is correct. Can we see evidence, for example, of a link between product innovation and superior performance? Or between customer service and customer loyalty?

The next step follows logically from the last one.

We need to define what actually causes the success to be achieved.

**What will *cause* the objective to be achieved?**

I call these causes of success the **Success Drivers**.

For example, if success is to generate a specific profit- or earnings-based measure, then we must identify those specific measurable Success Drivers that will cause it to be achieved.

Again, a simple example will illustrate the point.

## *Case example*

We know that for many corporations most of the profit tends to be derived from a few of the customers.

We know that customers are more likely to give the business to those suppliers that offer the greatest perceived added value. Now "added value" has become another of those clichés that are ill defined and can be used to mean many different things. For the purpose of this discussion, I want to keep it simple and say that by "added value" we will mean the customers' perception of the benefits received from the supplier in comparison to the price paid by the customer.

Let's assume that we are operating in a market where the products or services are fairly similar and where each of the suppliers sells at roughly the same price. A significant move in price by one of the suppliers would probably trigger a similar move from the others in order that they remain competitive and do not lose share and volume. This situation is typical for a great many market sectors.

Now there must be a link of some sort between the customers' perception of added value from a supplier and that supplier's sales. We may not know exactly what the link is, but it would be reasonable to believe that the link exists.

Therefore, the customers' perception of added value could, in this case, be a Success Driver. After all, if the price is similar, the product is similar and the quality and service are similar, how does the customer decide which supplier or suppliers to favor?

So if we use this example, we would make every effort to measure customer perception and to try to link the results to our own success. We would be looking for those few things within "customer satisfaction" that drive our own success.

## Most organizations do not know how their customers measure added value

This might sound like a very simple example and not very enlightening, yet an audit of a cross section of organizations revealed that 62% of those surveyed carried out no customer satisfaction or perception audits and 87% were unable to define specifically how their most important customers measured added value or how they rated their supplier's ability to deliver added value.

So what we are doing in this step is using the learning from the previous steps and identifying those Success Drivers that we can reasonably assume will cause the overall objective and in turn the secondary objectives to be achieved.

Of course they will be different for different organizations in different circumstances.

You can see now why the overall objective is so important. Not only do we ensure that everyone is working for the same result, but the specific Best Practice model and therefore the activities will be governed by the selection of the objective and so Success Drivers may not always be so obvious.

## There is more than one Success Driver

One of the lessons that some managers find hard to accept is that you cannot focus on just one Success Driver or assume that 100% achievement of that Success Driver is beneficial. For many people, this sounds counter-intuitive. If something is believed to be a Success Driver then surely a little bit "more" of the Success Driver must lead to more success. This sounds like a logical view. Sadly this may not be so.

It is important not to assume that there is a consistent relationship between Success Drivers and the achievement of the objective.

For example, most people would tend to include "Customer Satisfaction" as a Success Driver. The logic goes that the more satisfied the customer is, the more likely you are to get and retain the business. Once again this sounds logical but it may not always be the case.

It could be that Customer Satisfaction does not always impact the achievement of the overall objective. Other issues might cloud the picture.

## *Case study – A little bit more may not help at all*

Let's take another familiar example to illustrate the point. Every one of us will have a bank account. Suppose for a moment that you work for the bank and that you are responsible for maintaining the bank's customer loyalty. In other words, you want to ensure that the bank does not lose customers to competitive banks. You intuitively know that this means that your bank must offer a high standard of customer service yet you must be sure that you are not spending money and effort unnecessarily since this would damage your bank's profits. You also know that it is much more expensive to win a new customer than it is to retain an existing customer.

It is a reasonable assumption that customer loyalty is linked to customer satisfaction. The more satisfied a customer is, the more likely the customer is to remain with the bank, you might assume. You might conclude that there is a simple relationship between customer loyalty and customer satisfaction. If you were to draw a graph of the relationship in this case it might look like this.

The graph assumes a direct relationship between Customer Loyalty on the *y*-axis and Customer Satisfaction on the *x*-axis. Very high satisfaction produces very high loyalty and similarly very low satisfaction leads to very low loyalty. This is the logic that many service companies use.

Reality is rarely a straight line!

However, when you conduct the analysis, you might find that for your bank, the link between customer satisfaction and customer loyalty is not a straight-line relationship. You might find that the relationship looks a bit like this:

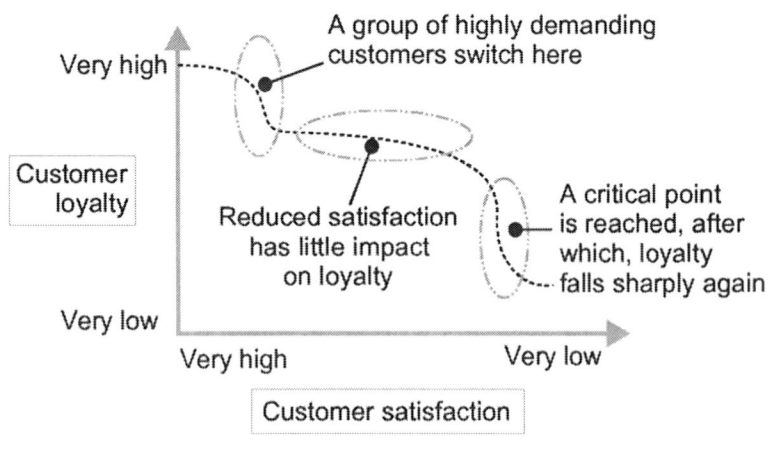

Far from being a straight line, you might see that the relationship between customer loyalty and customer satisfaction is a stepped curve, with an extended plateau at the center.

## What is happening?

You could attempt to interpret the curve, starting at the lop left, as follows.

A very small decrease in customer satisfaction has no impact on loyalty. Quite soon though we see that we reach a point where a group of highly demanding customers is likely to leave the bank for a competitor as soon as the service declines a little bit further. This might account for the first of the steps in the curve. But we find that the majority of customers are prepared to stay with the bank despite considerably worsening service until a critical point is reached when most of the customers switch, leaving a rump of totally loyal customers who seem oblivious to the level of service received. This might account for the extended plateau followed by the second step change.

## Why would this happen?

It might happen if there were issues in addition to service that influenced the customer. Suppose that the perceived difficulty of switching bank accounts was important to the customer. If the customer believed that switching accounts was just too difficult and caused too much trouble then he or she might be prepared to put up with poorer service from the current bank. This might continue for some time with ever worsening service and therefore satisfaction, until the situation became intolerable for most customers, at which point the poor service becomes more of an influencer than the perceived or actual difficulty of switching to another bank. A lot of customers might be prepared to switch at this point. Some commentators will define this as the "tipping point"; the point at which a little bit more makes all the difference. The straw that breaks the camel's back, if you prefer. Even so, there still seems to be a group of customers for whom even terrible service is not sufficient to persuade them to switch to a competitor in the same way that a small number of customers is only prepared to accept the very highest level of service.

## So what?

Well, if you were the manager responsible for customer loyalty and effective use of marketing funds for the bank, the money you could spend to improve customer service might have no impact at all on customer loyalty, or might have a dramatic impact. It would all depend upon the point at which your level of service was situated along the curve. So you can see that it is possible to find yourself in a situation where spending more money and effort on a defined Success Driver could have absolutely no impact. If you were not aware of the relationship between customer loyalty and customer service, you would be very concerned that your additional efforts to raise customer service had no impact on loyalty and you might conclude that the two were not connected at all.

I have found many similar situations where managers have concluded that certain actions or initiatives had no impact upon their business simply because they had not recognized that the relationship is not represented by a straight line. The relationship does exist but not in the way they expected. It is much more usual to find relationships expressed not as simple straight lines but as curves with various degrees of complexity.

In some cases the data will exist within the company to make an approximate plot of the relationship or, failing this, we could make at least a good guess and then conduct a number of field tests. The difficulty that the company could face, though, is a situation where there are multiple Success Drivers impacting the situation simultaneously. In this case plotting the possible relationships becomes very complex since different Success Drivers are likely to have different degrees of influence at different times. Most of the time we will rely on good guesswork and tests but in some cases the organization will need to have a more definitive answer. Here the company needs to turn to mathematical modeling techniques to resolve the issue. There are a number of possible techniques used; one of the most useful being Agent Based Modeling, but a review of them lies outside the scope of this book. A summary of Agent Based Modeling is included in the Appendix for those readers who are interested.

### The link between Success and Success Drivers may not be linear

Of course, the example here is simplified to make the point but we need to recognize that the relationship between the various critical Success Drivers and Success is unlikely to be a constant straight line. Effort placed on different Success Drivers at different times could have dramatically different results.

### Success Drivers – things to remember

Since we may not always have the data available, we cannot always easily measure directly the impact of the Success Driver, but you should recognize these fundamental issues.

- There will be a number of Success Drivers.
- You should be aware of the most critical Success Drivers.
- Each of them can be measured to some extent (don't forget – if you can't measure it, you can't manage it).
- Each is likely to be more or less important at different times.
- You should not pursue one at the expense of all the others all of the time.
- Pursuing any one Success Driver to 100% is unlikely to be cost effective.

So once again, what you want to do is identify those things that are most likely to cause success to happen and then consider their relative impact.

### Success Jargon

I use the term Success Driver because it is descriptive. In order to avoid any confusion, I should point out that different organizations might use different terms for Success Drivers. You may hear the following terms used instead:

- Key Performance Indicators (KPIs)
- Critical Performance Indicators
- Specific Local Objectives
- Role Specific Objectives
- Critical Success Indicators
- Scorecard Indicators
- Scorecard Measures

… and many others.

Each of these terms is similar and most are all but identical. What we are saying is that these specific measures are the ones that are critical to the organization in that they are the ones that are most likely to cause the fundamental objective (Success) to be achieved.

### Success Drivers tend to be hierarchical

We should also recognize that the Success Drivers can be hierarchical. I am going to use a very simple example to illustrate the point.

Returning to our earlier example, we will assume that we have determined that there is very likely to be a link between overall "Customer Satisfaction" and the sales we generate as a business, although we might not know the exact nature of the relationship. We may not know the shape of the relationship curve, for example. Therefore "Customer Satisfaction" is a Success Driver if the objective is expressed as Sales. We must then decide how we achieve the desired standard of "Customer Satisfaction" within the defined budget.

## *Case example*

Let's assume, for the purpose of our discussion, that we have determined that the frequency of customer contact has a direct bearing on the satisfaction of the customer. The more frequently we have contact with a customer, the more likely the customer is to be satisfied. In this case customer contact must also be a Success Driver.

We can depict this relationship in the form of a hierarchy.

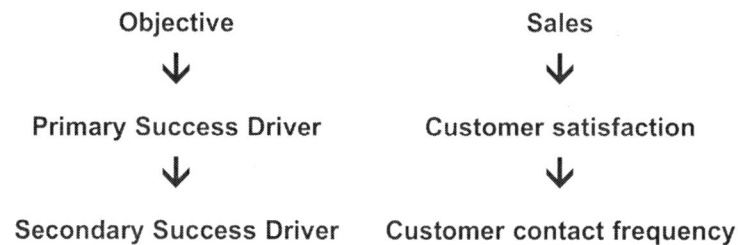

**Objective**                                **Sales**

↓                                ↓

**Primary Success Driver**          **Customer satisfaction**

↓                                ↓

**Secondary Success Driver**     **Customer contact frequency**

*Simplified example to demonstrate the hierarchy of Success Drivers.*
*In reality there will be many Success Drivers.*

This is just a simplified illustration. In reality, there will be many other Success Drivers to consider and there is a limit to the impact of customer contact. Presumably we would reach a point where our contacts are so frequent that they are having a detrimental effect upon our relationship with the customer. In our graph, we might see satisfaction declining at the extreme of contact frequency. In reality we would seek input from the customer as part of our routine Customer Perception and Benchmark analysis to determine the optimal type and frequency of customer contact.

The important point that I want to make is that there are likely to be additional Success Drivers 'below' each of the main Success Drivers.

## What will cause the Success Driver to happen?
The simplest way to think about this is, whenever you encounter a Success Driver, to ask yourself the following question:

**'What will cause this Success Driver to happen?'**

In other words, for our example the sequence would be:

**'What are the Success Drivers that cause sales?'**

We might have decided that one of the Success Drivers is 'Customer Satisfaction. So the next question is:

**'What causes 'Customer Satisfaction?'**

Our conclusion is that the customer contact frequency is one of a number of causes or drivers of Customer Satisfaction. Therefore we would want to define the optimal frequency and type of customer contact.

## Success Driver measures

Having established the sequence of Drivers, we can determine the measures. For example, what is the measure of customer satisfaction? How many customer contacts, of what type, in a period of time and with whom, are likely to contribute to the level of customer satisfaction that we need? What if the number of customer contacts deemed necessary exceeds our budget? What other Customer Satisfaction drivers could be used?

As an aside, there are a number of statistical analytical techniques that might be used to assist the company to answer some of these questions. For example, Conjoint Analysis seeks to compare the relative impact of different Drivers. Again a detailed discussion of mathematical modeling techniques lies outside the scope of this book but a summary of Conjoint Analysis is included in the Appendix.

To conclude the example, at the completion of this exercise we should have decided upon our general plan for customer contact. We should of course anticipate that we would want to amend this generic plan for specific customers. We do not want a process that is so rigid as to prevent good customer service!

Do not worry if you don't get it right the first time. None of us ever does! Best Practice development is all about trial and error and continually moving toward a better solution.

The important thing, as I will discuss later, is to measure the results and determine if our Success Driver targets are really having the right effect. If not, then we change them.

## Success Drivers in a nutshell

This idea of Success Drivers is in some ways a curious one in that some people accept it immediately while others find it difficult to see the value. It may seem complex but it all comes down to one simple point.

**If you are clear what you want to achieve (Success)
and you are clear about how to measure it,**

then,

**you need to define the few things that will cause Success
to happen. These are the Success Drivers.**

That is it.

## When in doubt – focus on the "cause"

If you are in any doubt about which Success Drivers are the right ones to use, you simply start with the objective and ask yourself: *"What will cause this to happen?"*

Then for each of the subsequent answers, ask again: *"What will cause this to happen?"*

... until you get to things that can be done.

## Not all of the Success Drivers will be obvious at the start

A final key point within this section, is that not all of the Success Drivers may be recognized at this stage. It may well be that we miss aspects that later are seen as important. We may also need to consider input from external sources, for example key customers over time, in order to develop our thinking further.

It is important to bear in mind that although this process is presented as a series of chronological steps, much of the time it tends to be an iterative process. We should not be concerned if we revisit a previous step in the light of new learning.

For example, it is quite common to add and amend the Success Drivers once we have considered in detail the activities of the top performers.

Quite often we find that an effective approach will involve addressing a number of issues simultaneously. We might be looking for Success Drivers, top performers and Activities at the same time rather than in discrete steps.

I have considered each of these steps separately here for ease of discussion.

## *Step 4 – Define the Success Drivers*

Ask yourself:

What are our Success Drivers?

How do we measure each one?

To what extent do we understand the relationship between the Success Driver and the achievement of the objective?

# Step 5 – synthesize the Best Practice model

So hopefully, by this stage you have identified all or at least many of the elements of Best Practice found within the organization.

The next step is to assemble or synthesize them into a draft Best Practice model. Again you do not need to be concerned if you have not got it exactly right. The most effective development occurs as lots of small stages rather than one giant leap. Part of the Best Practice process is to revise the model regularly to incorporate the latest learning and so you should expect to make regular changes.

## Continuous improvement

This is, after all, the principle behind the concept of continuous improvement. The idea is that while it is very difficult to get to be 100% better in a short time, it is always possible to get 1% better. So get 1% better 100 times in succession. In other words, aim to improve continuously. The process is never complete.

When we come to synthesize the model, we are simply assembling all of the elements of Best Practice that we have observed.

The idea is that we build up a comprehensive Best Practice model from all of the pieces that we have found. We then use this as our basic Best Practice model for everyone.

## Not everything can be replicated

However, you may well find that your analysis has revealed some elements that are simply not replicable.

Earlier, I used the issue of personality to explain some top performance. We may find that people with certain personal characteristics seem to be more successful in certain circumstances.

## *Case example – looking for the model*

For example, I once found a situation in the medical profession where patients overwhelmingly preferred certain types of doctor. For a short while we thought that we had discovered the start of a Best Practice model for the most effective doctor/patient relationship.

It did not take too long to discover that in fact, rather than finding a collection of characteristics to correlate with success, there was really only one. The more popular doctor in this particular situation was older than average and the patients too were predominantly older. In this situation, older patients tended to prefer older doctors. Later we looked at a university medical practice. Younger patients seemed to prefer younger doctors. Not much of a Best Practice model there!

Clearly we cannot change people's age or personal characteristics, nor do we want to.

However, we should ensure that elements of the model that we believe we have discovered can be used by others. To be extreme to make the point and use an example I have cited earlier, there is little point in building a model based on success in a metropolitan area to be used by people working in a remote hamlet.

We must ensure that we fully understand the limits of the effectiveness of the elements of Best Practice that we have found. We would like the elements of the model to be universal but we will probably find that there are boundaries or limitations.

### Limits to Best Practice sharing

A typical situation is in sharing Best Practice approaches across international borders. The same product, used by similar people may require a completely different Best Practice model in each country simply as a result of the different market place. A good example of this is the market for alcoholic drinks. The product may be identical throughout the world and the profile of drinker may be very similar but the widely differing markets, logistics and local legislation are likely to mean that one model cannot simply be used in another market without modification.

## *Case example – creating the right environment*

Here is another example just to make the point. A company found that it could manage its many small customers very effectively by telephone rather than by a personal visit. The telephone sales person was able to manage very many more customers and could offer a much more frequent contact than was possible using the traditional approach. The company established a revenue limit above which it was decided that the customer should receive a personal call from a member of the field sales force. To encourage the telephone sales team, a generous bonus plan rewarded sales growth. So far everything looks sensible. But wait –

The most successful telephone sales people discovered all sorts of approaches to support the customer and grow the business. Exactly the ideas we would want to capture for the Best Practice model. However as soon as a customer reached a defined level of revenue, he or she was automatically reassigned to the field sales team. The telephone sales person lost the bonus opportunity and the results of all the hard work. The best telephone sales people suffered most.

The result was that the best telephone sales people had a strong incentive to ensure that the customer's revenue stayed below the point at which the customer would move to field sales and of course no one was interested in discussing best practice telephone sales techniques.

## Synthesizing Best Practice

Although the approach is presented as a chronological series of steps, I have already made the point you should expect to return to the early steps and that you should consider the early process as a number of iterations rather than a single linear process. It is likely that you may see Steps Three (Define the Best Practice Activity) and Four (Define the Success Drivers) as one process and that you may also find that you will question your initial thinking about top performance as you progress. In a few cases you may even want to revise your view of what Success (Fundamental Objective) actually should be. You should not be concerned if you need to revisit your thinking and question your initial ideas. This is especially so when there are deeply ingrained ideas about the organization that will be challenged.

As the analysis proceeds you will find that you are steadily building up a picture of what current Best Practice looks like. In other words the things that the top performers actually do and the way in which they do it. In turn this knowledge will help to define the systems, tools and skills that are required for the current Best Practice process. So what you will be constructing is a draft model for Best Practice. The model will be a synthesis of all of the pieces of apparent Best Practice that have been derived through analysis and observation. In some cases you may find that you have conflicting pieces in which cases you will want to go back to the source to re-assess the activities and assumptions.

You will also have identified a series of Success Drivers, those things that can be shown to cause success to happen. We will use some or all of these as part of the measuring system. Some people will refer to these measures as a Scorecard or as Critical Success Factors.

## Summarizing the synthesized Best Practice model

We have now reached the point where you will bring each of the pieces together to form one coherent process or series of processes. There are a number of methods for representing a Best Practice model but I prefer the flow chart approach because it is simple.

All you have to do is to depict each of the core elements of the process as a box connected to other boxes each representing other elements. Beneath the boxes defining the core elements you can note the tools, skills and so on that are used. I will use a simple example to illustrate the approach.

## Best Practice model – illustration

Let's consider that we are defining a Best Practice process to handle incoming calls. The background is that there has been a rising number of complaints about calls not being returned, the difficulty of getting to the right person and having to repeat the message to different people. At the same time, there is a concern internally that the call reception is not very efficient. We will assume that different individuals and groups have developed different approaches and that some of these approaches seem to attract far fewer complaints and require fewer people for less time. This is perceived to be top performance. As a result of the analysis of what the top performers actually do, a draft model has been defined. The model is illustrated below as a single flow but we need to recognize that this model has been derived from a number of different individuals and groups each doing different things. No one person or group is currently operating in the form described.

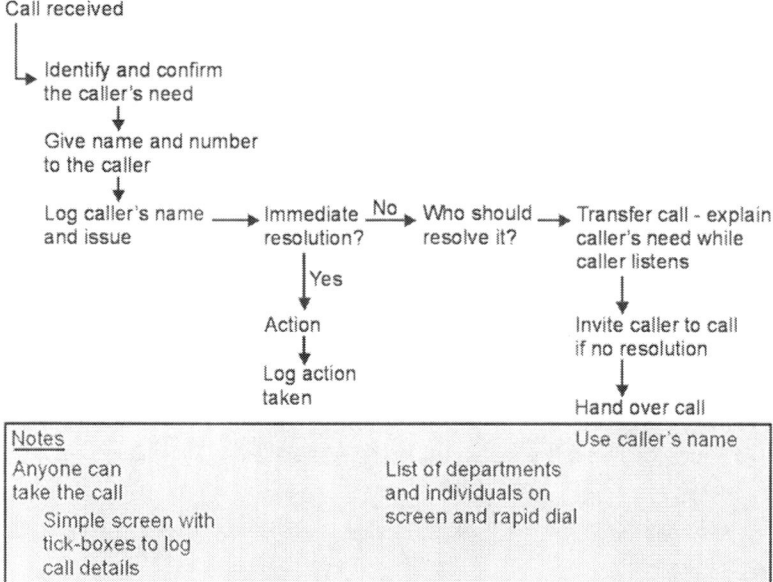

Call received
 └→ Identify and confirm
    the caller's need
        ↓
Give name and number
to the caller
        ↓
Log caller's name ——→ Immediate —No→ Who should ——→ Transfer call - explain
and issue              resolution?      resolve it?       caller's need while
                          │Yes                            caller listens
                       Action                                    ↓
                          ↓                             Invite caller to call
                       Log action                       if no resolution
                       taken                                     ↓
                                                        Hand over call

Notes                                        Use caller's name
Anyone can                      List of departments
take the call                   and individuals on
   Simple screen with           screen and rapid dial
   tick-boxes to log
   call details

What we have here is a simple illustration of a working document being used to define the initial part of the call handling procedure for a particular organisation. Note that this is not a general or generic recommended model. It is a model specific to one organisation. What works for one organisation may not work for another.

In this case, we see the main elements of the model and below a few notes which offer more information, answer an anticipated question and indicate a need to develop or adopt a tool.

Eventually the model will be developed with more detail and perhaps examples but, for now, this simple flow chart with accompanying notes will work perfectly well. It will be used to discuss the draft model with the practitioners. We may find that it will be refined further and that additional notes and detail will be added as the model is discussed.

This 'sense checking' of the model is the next step in our process.

## *Step 5 – Synthesize the Best Practice model*

Ask yourself:

---

Have we assembled all of the best practice elements into one single model?

_____

_____

_____

---

Are we sure that this really does represent Best Practice?

_____

_____

_____

_____

---

Are we sure that the model's components can be used by everyone throughout the organization?

_____

_____

_____

---

## Step 6 – Sense-check the model

So now we have the draft of a Best Practice model. The model has been put together based on the findings of the audit team. You will recall that our recommendation is to use people who are not well acquainted with the processes, since they are least likely to make assumptions and most likely to be objective.

## The audit team

The audit team will combine all of the elements of Best Practice, as they found them, into one comprehensive model. The team will ensure that the components selected will be applicable for everyone. They will also ensure that the components are capable of being replicated. For example if the most effective practitioners all have more than five years experience, this is interesting but not something that we can replicate across the whole team. We cannot suddenly give people more experience although we can share the benefits of that experience.

In some cases, building the model is a simple exercise of linking the various elements and processes, as we saw in the example above. In other cases, we may find that aspects of what we believe are Best Practice are in conflict. In this case, the audit team need to go back to those specific issues and look again. If it is still not possible to determine the issue, then we will ask the top performers themselves for a view when we review the model with them. We shall discuss this in just a moment.

## Visualizing the model as a flow chart

In most cases, I find that the best way to think about the model is as a flow chart. As you have seen, we construct the model so that each core step of the process will be represented by an icon or a box on the flow chart. The flow chart shows the connections, the relationships and the sequence of events. Each step of the process may then be sub-divided into mini processes. The requirements of each step will be defined, such as for example, the tools that should be used. If specific skills to a certain level are important, then they too will be defined.

What this should produce is a blueprint for the Best Practice model.

## Sense check with the practitioners

The next step is to present and test the model with the top performers. We do this in order to "sense check" the model with the experts to ensure that the results are accurate and realistic. Have we really understood what seems to be happening? This is also the time to discuss aspects of the process that appear unclear, are in conflict or simply need more discussion.

This part of the process is normally in the form of a seminar. At the start, the audit team present their view of the combined Best Practice process. The top performers or practitioners then have the opportunity to comment on and question the draft model. This is the time when changes can be made, further Best Practice uncovered and issues resolved.

The objective is to get agreement from the whole group about the Best Practice process. The model that results from this session is the one that will be implemented across the group.

Once again do not be excessively concerned about getting it 100% right the first time. There will be opportunities for further change later. I have already made the point that ongoing change should be part of the development program. I will be discussing the importance of regular review and change later on.

Assuming that the audit team has done a comprehensive job and has addressed the issues in sufficient detail, you will find that this step is straightforward.

Occasionally the practitioners will want to make amendments or to add some detail but in the main they will be in agreement. After all, it is their processes that have been summarized although perhaps not in one comprehensive process.

At the end of this step, we have a model that we are confident represents Best Practice as it exists within the organization at the moment.

## Step 6 – Sense check the model
Ask yourself:

> Are we confident that we have really summarized Best Practice as it exists at the moment within the business?

Are we sure that this process can be implemented across the whole organization?

_____

_____

_____

## Step 7 – Build the Best Practice model

The main task now is to take the model that is currently in the form of a flow chart and turn it into a process that can be implemented by the whole group.

Clearly this step is as critical as any other. Identifying Best Practice will be a purely academic exercise if you do not achieve any commercial advantage from it. The only way to make this happen is to get the model into use.

What you need is an implementation "kit" or process that will explain to the whole group how the new processes work and that will provide the various tools and systems that will be used.

Now the good news is that we are not starting from scratch. We should have at least the prototype for the implementation process already prepared to some extent, since we will simply be replicating processes that are already being used. We often find that the top performers are very useful in putting forward ideas to support the implementation since they are familiar with it. While we cannot just ask the top performers to specify the Best Practice process, we can ask them to define how they deal with specific issues, which tools they use and so on.

**The main components**
The main components of the implementation process are:

- an explanation of why we are doing it
- a summary of the Best Practice results compared to the average results – focus on the process not the people

- a summary of the new processes and components
- a detailed discussion about how the new process should be used
- an example of each of the tools that will be used
- a training process to teach the new process and skills if necessary.

Let's consider each of these components in turn.

## Explain why we are doing it

A core consideration in building and implementing the model is that we are requiring change. Later on, we shall discuss why initiatives like this tend to fail and we will see that top of the list is a reluctance to change. No one likes it and few really want it. We all feel most comfortable with what we know now.

So job number one is to explain why we are doing what we are doing. You will find that there will be a great many people in the organization who are perfectly satisfied with things as they are. They are sure that they are working as hard as possible now and that in general things are about as good as they will ever be.

And then you arrive telling them that John and Jane have found a better way and consequently everyone will have to change!

## Win the hearts and minds

Unless we can win over the hearts and minds of the majority, we will find it difficult to implement the plan.

I have found that the best way to begin is to take the time to explain the purpose of the exercise. What may seem obvious to you may well be novel and radical to someone else.

The recommended (Best Practice) approach to explaining any form of change is to start with what is commonly known. In other words begin with a common point that everyone will accept. Examples include the increasing competition, globalization effects, new technologies and so on. If the group has direct experience of these issues, then so much the better. Starting off on common ground will help to put everything else into perspective. People will start to see that this is not change for its own sake but as a result of a real issue that is impacting them.

## Sell the benefits

The next step is to explain that no-change is not an option. A good way to do this is to point out the likely circumstances that will arise if we do nothing. Generally the projection will indicate some worsening in the organization's position in some way and in particular a less effective competitive position. Our aim here is to demonstrate that simply continuing with the current approach, even though it has stood us in good stead up till now, can no longer be an option. We need people to get to this point before we move on. If everyone recognizes that the circumstances have changed, that consequently their situation will deteriorate in some way and that as a result they need to make some sort of change, then the implementation is much more likely to be accepted.

The question in people's minds should now be what to do rather than why do it.

## Explain how it works

So the next step is to explain the "what." Once again, it's a matter of how you tell it. No one wants to hear that another person or another group is smarter. Therefore we do not want to present the Best Practice model as John's or Jane's or head office's. In fact we want it to belong to everyone rather than be associated with any one group. And we certainly do not want it to be presented as the "consultants' solution!"

If we can present the comparative results between the Best Practice approach and the traditional approach, it is better not to attribute the results to any one person or team but rather to present them as "the results." It is generally helpful to convince everyone that the new model offers a superior approach if possible.

## Describe the approach

Once we have shown that there is a better way, the next step is to describe the approach. We divide this into two parts; the summary of the process to put everything into context followed by the more detailed discussion.

It is the detailed part that will describe the activities in depth. We need to ensure that everyone has complete clarity about what they will be required to do, how they do it, what tools and support are available and how they will be measured.

The "kit" itself usually takes the form either of a process to be used by the line manager and/or a self-teaching kit complete with examples.

The actual implementation phase is dominated by a series of seminar training sessions during which everyone gets ample opportunity to practice the new processes, use of tools and skills. In some cases, new skills will be required and there will be a need to instigate a training process.

## Step 7 – Build the Best Practice model
Ask yourself:

What should the model look like?

Am I confident that the model is comprehensive?

> How should we present the model to ensure that it will be accepted?
>
> _____
>
> _____
>
> _____

## Step 8 – Implement the Best Practice model

The actual implementation should be simply a matter of managing the plan that was developed in the previous step.

### Support from the top

The implementation will take the form of an explanation of the need followed by a discussion of the process detail. For a large program, the explanation of the reason for the program will be made by the General Manager. A more modest program will be introduced by the local senior manager.

### Constant follow up

One of the most important aspects of the implementation is follow up. We must not expect instant acceptance and understanding simply because people have attended a seminar. One of the classic mistakes made in any form of training is to assume that because people have attended a training seminar that they are now fully familiar with everything and that they are using everything that was presented. A much better approach is to see the seminar as simply the introduction and that the learning will be consolidated during a series of follow up sessions and most importantly on the job reinforcement.

The program must include frequent follow up sessions for individuals and for the groups. These sessions allow for feedback from the team and for further explanation as necessary. They also allow for plenty of role-play and practice.

## Maintain the momentum

An important aspect is to maintain the momentum that will be created at the start. One effective way of doing this is to identify and share early successes of the new approach. This has the effect of confirming the logic of the model and encouraging the group as well as building confidence.

It is important that success is identified and shared with the whole team. For this reason part of the process needs to include a mechanism to identify successes and to share the results with everyone. It is also useful if there is some sort of reward system for those people demonstrating success.

## Get everyone involved

It is a well-documented fact that people are more likely to be supportive when they feel part of the program and when they feel special. One of the tasks of the implementation team is to create an environment that fosters this feeling.

## Sometimes we will test the model

In some cases, we find that it makes sense to test the implementation of the model in one part of the organization before we roll it out.

We might do this if we were not completely confident about some aspects of the model or if we wanted to demonstrate to the doubters that the new model will yield better results than the current process.

Normally the model would be implemented as normal in a discrete part of the organization. We use the rest of the organization as the control.

Assuming that all goes well, then following the test phase, the model would be rolled out across the whole organization, using the superior results gained from the test.

## *Step 8 – Implement the Best Practice model*
Ask yourself:

> What are we doing to maintain the enthusiasm of the group?

> What is the process for follow up?

> How do we ensure that the new model becomes that normal way of doing things?

## Step 9 – Measure the results

A fundamental aspect of the model and its implementation is measurement.

We must not lose sight of the fact that the whole point of the exercise is to put ourselves into a stronger position to achieve the overall organizational objective. In this discussion, I have been calling this "Success" and those things that cause success to happen we have called the "Success Drivers."

The Best Practice model is simply intended to give us the best opportunity to achieve what we have defined as Success. It is not an objective in its own right. Implementing a Best Practice model that has no impact on the Success Drivers is a complete waste of time. Actually it is worse than a waste of time because it will also be a waste of money and so *reduce* the profitability of the organization.

So it is important that we build in measures to ensure that the results we want are likely to occur.

If the desired results are observed, then all is well. The task is to continue to maintain the momentum. This is the outcome of most Best Practice models.

However occasionally we find that there is no appreciable impact on the overall objective (Success) or on the Success Drivers.

There are a number of possible reasons for this:

## Time to have an impact on the Success Drivers

It may take some time to have an impact on the Success Drivers. If you suspect that this might be the case, then you need to identify some additional measures that will in turn impact the Success Drivers. You must have measures that will be affected by the new process. Without them it is a bit like flying a plane without instruments. You know you are moving but you are not sure if you are moving in the right direction and at the right speed.

## The model is wrong

It is possible, but unlikely, that the model is wrong. It is unlikely because it has been based on the very things that appear to be having the best effect within the organization.

## The model is not being implemented properly

Much more likely is that the model is not being implemented as planned. In my experience, this is undoubtedly the most common cause for failure. The problem occurs because a number of people either do not see the need for change or just do not want to use the new model for some reason. This is why the planning and implementation steps are so important.

## The circumstances have changed

I have encountered a few situations where the situation and circumstances change significantly. In this case the model is unlikely to be as effective. The remedy in this situation is likely to involve re-building the model from first principles. I discuss this approach later.

So the key point is that we need to establish measures that will indicate that the new model is having the desired impact. We need to select measures that will register fairly quickly so that we can all have confidence that the approach is working. Once again having early success and being able to demonstrate positive impact is important as part of the ongoing internal "selling" process.

## *Step 9 – Measure the results*

Ask yourself:

| Have we included the right measures? |
|---|
| |
| |
| |
| |

| Have we set targets for the measures? |
|---|
| |
| |
| |
| |

Have we identified the sources of early success?

_____

_____

_____

_____

Have we established a method of sharing success?

_____

_____

_____

_____

## Step 10 – Revise the model in the light of new learning and experience

Although this is the last step in our sequence, this is not the final step of the process. I have made the point a number of times that implementing the Best Practice approach is an ongoing process. An often-heard cliché would describe it as a journey rather than a destination.

There are a number of reasons why we should expect the process to change.

### The process is likely to change

It is unlikely that we captured the complete Best Practice process in the initial model. This will become clear as we implement and work with the model. Gaps will be discovered, areas of confusion and conflict will arise and they will be corrected. Provided the attitude is the right one and that we have led people to expect change, this should not prove to be a problem.

## Evolution will continue

We will also find, as we have discussed earlier, that individuals and groups will continue to identify new and better approaches and techniques. We should encourage this. A number of organizations have included a regular formal review of their various Best Practice models. For example, one organization runs an annual seminar in which each of the Best Practice models in use is re-assessed in some detail, in the light of experience and new learning. Each group is expected to arrive with improvements to the existing model along with an estimate of the impact that the improvements will have on the Success Drivers. In this way, the whole organization is expecting some change at least once every year. Some of the changes put forward are simple while others can be radical.

## The circumstances will change

Another reason to revise the model is that the circumstances will change. You will recall that in the early part of the book I made the point that today's model is unlikely to be as effective tomorrow. In other words we should expect to see the model evolving to reflect the changing environment in which we find ourselves along with the new and better techniques that we discover.

# Step 10 – Revise the Model in the light of new learning and experience

Ask yourself:

What is our process to ensure that the Best Practice model remains up to date?

_____

_____

_____

How do we ensure that we capture the latest learning?

_____

_____

_____

_____

How should we formalize the review process?

_____

_____

_____

_____

# 5

## Developing a Best Practice Approach by Importing Learning from Outside the Organization

There will be many situations where it makes more sense to import the basis of the Best Practice model from outside the organization. The difference between this approach and the previous one is that here you are likely to avoid much of the internal examination.

**You are likely to favor this option when:**

- you are not convinced that you have all of the elements of Best Practice within the organization
- there is likely to be a better approach or components of a better approach outside – in other words you can improve your current model by incorporating aspects of an external model
- another organization has already discovered and developed a clearly better approach – you should note that this better model might have been developed by an organization in a completely different market sector to your own
- you need to move quickly and do not want to spend the time looking for an internal solution.

**Benefits of using an external solution include:**

- the model is already developed and tested

- the model is ready now
- you can move much more quickly
- you do not have to invest the management time and effort to develop the model – although you will have to adapt the external model to suit your own circumstances.

### Concerns when using an external solution

- The external model must still be tailored to your own unique circumstances – very rarely can it be implemented without some work.
- The external model may not capture some of the unique aspects or subtleties of your situation.
- Some of your internally developed processes may actually be superior to the external model.
- There may be aspects of your internal processes that are critical to your organization but that are not considered in the external model.
- The model's acceptance by your management team may be more difficult since it was "not invented here" – on occasions the management team will simply not accept that anything from outside their organization could possibly be applicable.

## Don't reinvent the wheel

Despite these concerns, many organizations favor the external model approach, finding it much faster and offering the opportunity to bring in new processes that have not evolved within the organization. The feeling is that the proven external model offers a strong base for further development and refinement. Many managers are concerned that looking within the organization to develop a model may simply waste time developing what may already exist outside. No one wants to re-invent the wheel. There is a good argument for taking what has already been developed and applying your management time to taking this model a step further.

Experience suggests that there is a difference in perception between those organizations that seek to develop a Best Practice model from within and those that look outside. Organizations that look outside tend to be aware of a gap, real or perceived, between the effectiveness of their operation and activities and that of other organizations. In other words there is a stronger belief that there is a need for improvement.

Those organizations that look inside tend not to see such a gap. They tend to believe that they are at least as good as the majority and probably have little to learn from the outside. Their desire is to share the internal knowledge to enable the whole organization to become even more effective.

It is quite common to find the organizations that look outside for the basis of their model have had their need triggered by a particular event. A new senior manager, the results of a customer perception review, commercial results below expectations have all triggered a search for a more effective operation. These organizations tend to have a belief that they must improve in some way and that the improvement must happen quickly. There tends to be a stronger need for action and therefore change.

## Understanding Best Practice from outside our current operation

What we are doing here is taking either a complete Best Practice model or at least the skeleton of the Best Practice model that has already been developed by an organization in a similar position and adapting it for our own use.

### The external model is likely to have three possible sources

### 1)   A generic Best Practice model developed by a third party derived from studying a number of organizations

This developed model is intended to represent, so far as possible, the "best of the best" practice. It will have been developed by a third party organization that has expertise in the industry but does not represent any single organization. The third party organization may be funded by an industry group, a government sponsored body or by a commercial organization. In the first two situations, the results are usually made available to the participating organizations. In the last case, an organization can purchase the knowledge. Often a number of organizations will have pooled their efforts to determine a model.

This approach is often favored because it represents a comprehensive Best Practice process. In other words, an amalgamation of the Best Practice thinking across a number of organizations and management teams.

This approach assumes of course that there is a consensus approach and this is more likely to occur in a more mature market or environment. In a newer or rapidly changing market or environment where there are likely to be various different and possible conflicting approaches being used, this approach is less useful in that there may not be a consensus view. However we may find that an organization has sought to benchmark a few leading organizations to derive the start of a Best Practice model.

The idea of Benchmarking is often a useful one to consider. Here one or more organizations will consider all or part of a process and will share their thoughts and ideas with each other. Clearly there are issues concerning competitive practice and non-disclosure and so it is more usual to find similar but non-competing organizations participating in this sort of process. Once again, using a neutral third party organization has been found to be useful since now sensitive information can be collected and shared.

As an example, a recent survey on behalf of manufacturers in a specific sector considered the costs of various cooperative promotional activities with retailers. A neutral third party organization prepared a questionnaire to be completed by each participating manufacturer. Each manufacturer sent their sensitive information to the third party, which consolidated the results but did not identify each company. Thus all the participating manufacturers received a copy of the data from every other company but did not know which company had submitted which data. The results were particularly revealing to those manufacturers which believed they had negotiated a strong agreement with the retailer only to find that other manufacturers had been given a much more generous deal. If this approach is considered, attention must be given to the local and regional competitive legislation. We have found that activities that are acceptable in one country are not acceptable in another.

## 2) A single model that has been developed by one other organization

This situation typically arises when one, usually large and often international organization, has developed a process that is perceived as offering greater benefits than the more traditional approach.

It is likely to be preferred as a method of developing a Best Practice model when:

a) a senior manager moves from one organization to another.

This manager may have been hired as a result of achieving impressive results with another organization. The manager is likely to bring an established process and approach that represents Best Practice for the previous organization.

b) one organization takes over another or when two or more organizations come together.

It is not unusual to find that even in an apparent "merger," one of the organizations tends to dominate. Often, one organization will want to impose its own processes and systems on the other although I have also found situations where the dominant company has adopted processes from its smaller "partner."

As an aside, an alternative approach to developing a Best Practice model for the new organization following a merger or acquisition, that I find is generally more successful, is to use the approach discussed earlier, to develop a model from the combined internal processes. In this case though, we would consider building a single model for the merged organizations by assessing current processes in both organizations. This approach has the added benefit of helping the merger process produce one coherent organization, a goal that many merged organizations struggle to attain in the short or even medium term.

A concern often expressed by the management team is that the organization will simply replicate another organization's model and in doing so will lose any aspects of its own competitive advantage. The response to this point is that any model must be adapted to meet the specific needs and situation. By using another's model, you could say that you are putting yourself at the same level in order to add your own unique aspect to generate your own competitive edge. The smart way to do it is to take the best from outside your organization and to add your own unique elements and so create a model that is superior. A number of large corporations from the Far East and South East Asia have used this approach very successfully.

3)  **A model aimed at replicating the approach of one or more organizations. This may have been gained by studying these, potentially competitive, organizations but without the agreement of the organization being studied.**

A similar but slightly different approach is for an organization to learn from approaches developed by competitive organizations. The main difference is that the organization being studied is not participating in the analysis since it is very unlikely, and in some cases it may be illegal, for a competitive organization to share its learning. The trick is to assess the results of Best Practice achieved by the competitive organization and to make educated judgements about the processes used. Some organizations have built this approach into their normal competitive analysis and intelligence collecting process and may go through this exercise on a regular basis.

There are a number of sources of information for the organization taking this approach. Customers provide a very good source of information. Customer perception assessments and supplier bench-marking analyses will reveal a great deal of useful information. Customers are normally willing to compare the performance of a number of suppliers both quantitatively and qualitatively and to discuss the approaches taken by different suppliers from the customer's point of view. In a similar way the organization can study the results obtained by a competitor in other visible areas.

For example, one of the most obviously visible areas for any organization that markets its products through a retail environment is the point of sale. We can observe the way that a competitor seeks to market and position its product simply by visiting the various stores. Logistics and supply chains are often fairly visible also as are customer support systems and marketing initiatives. This approach is of course not a new one. Product development teams have been studying competitors' products and using the technique of reverse engineering to understand how a competitor is producing its products for many years.

Of course, what we are often observing are the results of the Best Practice model, rather than the complete model itself. This, though, may be enough. If we know that a competitor is achieving improved results and we can observe a change in the way the point of sale, for example, is managed, then we can probably deduce the basis of the method. This should be enough for us to consider the benefits, if any, in our adapting our own approach to resemble their new approach.

Another good source of competitive information is third parties in the route to market. Distributors, agents and wholesalers can provide useful information either directly or indirectly through observation.

## The external model must still be adapted

Wherever we get our external model from, we must still adapt it to fit our own circumstances. It would be unusual to be able to implement the external model without some change. This is because every organization is unique is some way. The model from the outside will contain elements that may not reflect our situation and may contain elements that are surplus for us.

Whatever the source of the external model, the task is to consider the model in the light or your own situation and then to establish the difference between the model and your current activities.

Best Practice

As before, we can consider a series of 10 essential steps that you should work through.

## The 10-step approach to developing Best Practice from an external source

As with my approach to developing the Best Practice model from within, the process of building the Best Practice model by starting with an external model, follows a similar 10-step process.

The first step is identical. As you would expect, the most fundamental issue is to agree and confirm exactly what your organization wants to achieve and the measure it will use to judge its success. In other words, what is your fundamental objective?

The next two steps require you to identify the source of your external model and to define the model itself. You will then need to consider the Success Drivers that are most applicable. You may well have your own version of the Success Drivers but you will certainly want to challenge them. It may be that the external model will alter your view about the Success Drivers and their relative importance. For this reason, Step 2 of the process is to identify the external model and Step 3 looks at the components of the external model. It is Step 4 where you define the revised Success Drivers for your own organization.

In the process that considered the internal Best Practice model we were assuming that you already have the main component of Best Practice within your organization and that the task is to identify these components and consequently define the model. Therefore we were able to identify the Success Drivers at the start.

When we are importing the Best Practice model we may find that we have not defined all of the Success Drivers or that we want to amend the Success Drivers and we will use the learning from the external model to help us.

In other words the external model is likely to influence our choice of Success Drivers. For this reason, you may find that you change the Success Drivers as you move through the process.

The final steps, involving building the detail, implementing and measuring the model are similar to the previous process.

# The 10-step approach to developing Best Practice from an external source

| Step 1 | Define Success |
|--------|----------------|
| Step 2 | Identify the external source of the model |
| Step 3 | Define the external model |
| Step 4 | Define the Success Drivers |
| Step 5 | Compare the external model to the current operation and identify the differences |
| Step 6 | Design the revised model (the blend of the external with your retained elements) |
| Step 7 | Build the detail for the revised model |
| Step 8 | Implement the revised model |
| Step 9 | Measure the results |
| Step 10 | Revise the model in the light of new learning and experience |

## Step 1 – Define success

Follow the same process that was described in the previous section.

## Step 2  – Identify the external source of the model

There are a number of potential sources for the external learning.

Most of the time the source will be defined by default.

## New managers

The most obvious source is provided when a new senior manager joins the organization having had direct experience of other approaches. The benefit here is that the new manager should be intimately acquainted with the external model and so no time is required to conduct analysis or investigation. The organization will however still need to ensure the new model will meet the needs and own unique situation. It is likely that you will need to amend and adapt the new model to some degree.

## Competitor models

A number of organizations have decided to base all – or more usually part – of their model on a competitor. This is typically the case where an organization believes that the competitor has a clearly superior approach and as a result is achieving a competitive advantage. Of course, you cannot just go and ask the competitor how the model works. What you can do is to make educated guesses by observing the results of the activity. You can also learn a great deal by talking with mutual customers and customers served by the competitor and third parties in the route to market. Generally I find that customers and potential customers are prepared to discuss supply issues and to assist you to benchmark suppliers. You can also learn a certain amount simply by reading the publications produced by the competitive organization, including the annual report. Once again, the general intent can be interpreted using educated guesswork. A further resource is provided by third party industry reports, which may consider the strategies and approaches of the major players. Of course if you are in a non-competitive environment, charity work or fundraising for example, then it may be much easier to talk with similar local organizations that may be quite happy to share their ideas with you.

If you do not have any form of formal competitive intelligence and information gathering process then it would be well worth considering this as part of your normal ongoing operation.

## Non-competing organizations

Some organizations are wary of trying to base a Best Practice model on a known nearby competitor. The reluctance stems from two concerns. The first is that you can never learn the sufficient level of detail about the competitor's system to be able to replicate it and that even if you could, it would only put you level. What these managers are seeking is a model that offers the chance for their organizations to surpass the competitor. One way of approaching this issue is to form development partnerships with non-competing but similar organizations or at least organizations facing similar issues. These might be found in your own market or it may make good sense to look to international markets. You may well find an organization that looks very similar to your own and that faces very similar issues in another market. It may be that this organization has already gained extra learning or even developed its own Best Practice model that it would be prepared to share. Usually these relationships involve some form of quid pro quo and in some cases can develop into formal or semi formal strategic relationships.

As an example of this approach in the not-for-profit sector, a number of the world's opera houses have shared ideas and the results of initiatives with respect to ticket pricing, subscription pricing and developing audience loyalty. Each opera house faces very similar issues, has the same "product" yet given their geographic diversity do not compete for the same individual audience member.

## Third parties

An increasingly prevalent approach is to work with a third party that has developed a generic or an industry specific model. Normally this model will have been developed by studying a number of organizations that are seen as the most successful. The model itself will be a generic model and so must be adapted to the specific needs of the organization yet should contain the common core elements developed to a reasonable degree. A clear benefit of this approach is that the basic model is less likely to be geared to one organization only and is likely to include the best learning from a number of organizations. Third parties may also be useful in providing industry or sector data that can be used to provide benchmark figures.

When considering other organizations or sectors to provide a model for you, don't confine yourself only to looking at very similar organizations. I have found that great learning can be achieved by looking at organizations that may be from very different market sectors yet share similar issues.

Examples that I have used include the following:

- building supplies and pharmaceuticals
- short life perishable foods and radioactive medical products
- computer and electronic goods production systems and supermarket logistics and supply processes

### Consider the source before you start

It is well worth spending some time at the very start of the Best Practice project as a management team to consider potential sources of a Best Practice model. A good way to start the process is to consider those organizations that you would like to emulate. If you cannot think of any, then perhaps your model lies within your organization. Most often the results of this line of thinking include a synthesis of various elements of different organizations. The next step is to define the desired results more formally. This provides a clear direction and sense of outcome to everyone.

### *Step 2 – Identify the external source of the model*

Ask yourself:

| Which organizations would you most like to emulate? |
| --- |
|   |
|   |
|   |
|   |

What advantages would your organization gain?

_____

_____

_____

_____

Are there any generic industry models available?

_____

_____

_____

_____

## Step 3 – Define the external model

Having identified the source or sources of the external model, the next step is to define the model in some detail. The detail needs to be sufficient so that the model is capable of being considered in relation to the organization and its current approaches, the changes required and the process for implementation.

When I talk about defining the external model, what I mean is establishing the fundamental mechanisms and processes of the model. You need to be able to describe the way in which the new model works; what happens, who does what, what skills and tools are required and so on.

### Use process flow charts

I generally find that process flow charts, as we discussed earlier, are the most effective way for describing the new model. The flow chart will detail not only the actions, but also the responsibilities, tools and so on. This approach provides a good way to explain to a group how the new model might work and to set the scene for debate and discussion.

## Case example – local rather than central supplies purchasing

For a simple example, let's consider a Best Practice model that defines the approach for purchasing departmental suppliers.

In the original model, all purchasing was the responsibility of a central purchasing department, which consolidated requests from each department. This was considered to be the most sensible way to manage the process. During the development of a Best Practice model, an organization discovered that another company had experienced significant cost saving by giving each local department its own budget and allowing the department to make its own purchases as necessary from whichever supplier it preferred. The central purchasing department was no longer required. Despite some initial internal concern, this approach was tested and then implemented throughout the organization as part of the new Best Practice model when the test revealed comparable savings.

This is an example of discovering and implementing a new approach where previously there was no perceived need to change. It was only when the potential savings and higher level of local satisfaction, brought about by a sense of local ownership, were discovered that the new process was considered.

Clearly it pays to be constantly looking for different approaches not because they will always be applicable to your organization but so that you can at least be aware of alternatives.

### Appraise the new model

One of the benefits of defining in some detail the external model that you intend to use is that you are disciplined to ensuring that you do fully understand the intended model and that all of the critical elements are in place.

So the idea is to be able to consider the external model with respect to the organization's objectives. The question is:

**Do we believe that the approach described by the new model will enable us to achieve our objectives?**

It is of course critically important to get this right. You do not want to implement a new process that does not support the achievement of your objectives. You must ensure that the process does not take precedence over the achievement of your own defined fundamental objective. The more similar your situation is to the situation of the organization(s) from which you have taken the model, then the more applicable the model is likely to be.

## The danger of assumptions in using external models

The key thing though is to question the rationale for each aspect of the intended Best Practice model. You should not assume that it must be right.

There is a story told of a newly married couple cooking dinner. Both the husband and the wife had a preferred method for preparing and cooking the roast beef. The husband was surprised to observe his wife cutting the ends off the beef before she placed it into the roasting pan. Thinking that this must be an improved cooking method with which he was unfamiliar, the husband asked his wife why she did this. His wife said that she did not know but this was what her mother had always done and so she was just following the "approved model." The wife called her mother to discover the reason. Her mother did not know either but said that she was following the example of her own mother. The wife then called her grandmother. Her grandmother explained that at the time she had a very small oven and roasting pan and was forced to cut the beef down to size in order to fit it into the oven. The point is that we need to question everything to convince ourselves that they really do meet our current needs rather than represent received wisdom.

At the end of this step you should have convinced yourself that the new model offers clear benefits over the current approach and that you are confident that it will give you the best chance of achieving your objectives.

The next step is to confirm the Success Drivers.

## *Step 3 – Define the external model*

Ask yourself:

Have you defined the basic process of the external model?

Have you defined the start and end points?

Have we identified which aspects of the model are currently in place?

# Step 4 – Define the Success Drivers

The previous discussion about Success Drivers still applies. You will recall that by "Success Drivers" we mean the very things that will cause success to happen.

The difference now is that we may find that the choice of Success Drivers will be influenced by the learning from the external model.

In some cases, you will find that the external model defines the specific measures or Success Drivers. This is likely to be the case when you use a comprehensive model that has been developed from observations of a number of organizations. In most cases we will find that the external model does indicate the core Success Drivers that should be used.

## Have we got the right Success Drivers?

The task is to ensure that these Success Drivers are indeed the ones that will cause your own objective to be achieved.

If your definition of success (your objective) is different from the other organization, it is almost certain that you will need to adapt the Success Drivers. It is of course critically important that you get the Success Drivers right since all of your activities will be directed to achieving them. You will also want to ensure that the relationship between your definition of success and the Success Drivers is clear.

As before, if you are in any doubt about which Success Drivers are the right ones to use, you simply start with the objective and ask yourself

### "What will cause this to happen?"

Then for each of the answers ask again,

### "What will cause this to happen?"

until you get to things that can be done.

Let's look at a simple example to indicate how the external model might influence the choice of Success Drivers.

## Case example – Success Drivers

A business-to-business manufacturer had a new CEO who was brought in with the aim of driving profitability. The CEO had in turn brought in a new CFO who had embarked upon a detailed review of all aspects of the organization and the business, the aim being to reduce waste and raise efficiency. One of the areas that the CFO had identified as requiring attention was the cost involved in servicing the customers. The concern was that many customers were too costly to maintain using the current approach. As part of the overall development initiative, the CEO was keen to identify and implement Best Practice models.

The manufacturer had traditionally employed a relatively large sales team to make direct calls on its customers. The manufacturer competed with three other companies, each having a very similar product range and operation. The market overall was static; any growth in the traditional market must come from taking share from a competitor. Launching new products was seen as expensive and risky and would only cannibalize the current product range. Consequently, the market was very price sensitive. The majority of the customer base was made up of small companies employing few people where the owner was also the manager and supervisor. The manufacturer's sales person would collect the customer's order and would support the customer with technical knowledge.

In order to reduce costs, the manufacturer's new CFO had assessed the customer base order patterns and had reduced the sales team and the sales team customer call frequency in line with the demand, thus reducing the overall cost of sale.

The paradigm maintained by the traditional management team within the manufacturer was that customer service through the personal visit of the sales person was the only real point of competitive advantage, given that there were few differences between the competitors' products, service or quality. This view was widely shared within the industry and hence the various competing manufacturers were determined to retain the frequency of the sales visits to the customer. Consequently, the new direction demanded by the CFO was not welcomed.

The manufacturers were amazed therefore when a foreign competitor entered the market with no field sales team. The new competitor imported the product and sold entirely through a dedicated telephone sales team.

The analysis conducted as part of the Best Practice study revealed that the customers were entirely familiar with the products and no longer required any technical support. The customers also wanted to reduce cost by reducing stock holding and so many preferred to place small frequent orders. Contrary to the view of the traditional manufacturers, the customers saw the sales visit as more of a hindrance than a help since it distracted the owner/manager from his or her work. The idea of being able to order by telephone or the Internet when they needed the order rather than when the sales person arrived, was much more attractive to the customers. But the real winner for the new foreign competitor was that it had a much lower cost of sale and could afford to pass on some of the saving to the customers without eroding its own margin.

The customer received a much better "service" at a lower price. Having deduced this lesson relatively early, the manufacturer was able to alter its route to market to compete directly with the new oversees competitor and to gain share quickly at the expense of its traditional and slower-witted competitors. A number of these competitors subsequently were forced out of business or sold out.

The lesson is that we need to ensure that we really are clear what drives our business and that the Success Drivers that were effective yesterday are still effective today.

You have to question your paradigms constantly – if you don't, someone else will and that someone else may be a new competitor. My experience is that the most vulnerable business is that one that sees no credible threat right now and sees no need to question its current operation or to consider any chance as necessary.

The history of business is full of stories of dominant corporations hanging on to previously successful paradigms and losing their share to new companies that have looked at the market with fresh eyes.

## *Step 4 – Define the Success Drivers*

Ask yourself:

> What evidence do we have to convince us that our paradigms are still correct?
>
> _____
>
> _____
>
> _____

> Are we sure that we have identified the Success Drivers?
>
> _____
>
> _____
>
> _____
>
> _____

> Are there lessons from outside our organization that might persuade us to change our Success Drivers?
>
> _____
>
> _____
>
> _____

## Step 5 – Compare the external model to the current operation and identify the differences

So far you have defined your own objectives, decided that you need to look outside the organization for the Best Practice model, identified one or more sources for the model and defined the basis of the model that you will use. In some cases, the model will be drawn together using the components from a number of models.

## Compare the model with current practice

You need to compare the new model with your current practice. You do not need to conduct a detailed analysis of your current operation; you just need to understand how close or far apart your current operation is from the new potential model.

In some areas, you may find that the new model is very similar to what you are currently doing, in other areas there will be small differences and in other areas again there will be such differences that you will need to discard the current processes in order to implement the completely new approach.

It is very important that you go through this exercise. The benefits will be seen later when you come to implement the new process. If people do not see the subtle differences between the new model and the current procedure than they are likely to assume they are the same and simply continue with the current operation.

## Blend the new and the old

We want to blend the two processes, the current process and the new model, into one seamless process that can be implemented across the whole team.

What we are looking for at this stage is to identify the aspects of the current operation that will be retained.

Many managers at this stage will argue that it is easier to forget the current operation completely and just implement the new model. While this approach is intellectually attractive, we have found that most people are more comfortable with the "new" model when it has elements with which they are already familiar. The idea of completely discarding a series of processes that have been used apparently successfully for a long period and replacing them with a series of seemingly untested processes is very concerning for many people.

## Don't throw away the good stuff!

So the recommendation is to use the current processes in their current or amended form wherever possible.

Of course in some cases the difference between the two approaches in simply too great and we just have to replace the current approach entirely.

The method of comparing the two approaches is, on the face of it, simple. The new model is presented to a group of practitioners. This team is asked to identify those aspects of the new model that currently exist and those elements of the new model that must be amended to conform to the unique situation. We may find for example that we want to retain one small element of the current process and to include it in the revised model.

## The new model really is "new"

There is an important issue to keep in mind here; some managers and practitioners have a tendency to claim that they are already operating to the "new" model; in other words that there is nothing "new" in the new model. Some managers will even claim that the new model is not new at all but is a description of the current procedure. We can all understand this reaction. Few people want to be told that their system that has worked perfectly well in the past is to be replaced by one developed by outsiders who have found a better way. As a result, what we sometimes see when the new model is presented is a manager claiming that all or parts of the model are already in place. In some cases of course, the manager may be right. So what we need is a simple way of sorting the genuine from the hype. The issue is to ensure that the organization does genuinely have the procedures that are being claimed.

The way we resolve this issue is to have the manager present the current process in detail. By detail I mean the actual processes along with completed examples and evidence that they are really used in this way. The detail will include the tools and measures and so on, in fact all of the aspects that have been summarized in the new model. In this way, everyone can see how much the current process really matches with the new process and how much really exists. Of course I will always explain that this will be the "acid test" at the start of the meeting before any claims are made! The idea is to keep everyone on the same side.

So at the conclusion of this step, you will have:

- identified which aspects of the new model currently already exist
- identified which parts of the current process can be amended easily to conform to the new model
- identified which aspects of the current model you want to retain and to incorporate in the new model.

The next step is to combine the new model with the existing processes and elements to produce a model that you believe represents a Best Practice approach for your unique situation.

### Step 5 – Compare the external model to the current operation and identify the differences

Ask yourself:

What evidence do we have to convince us that our paradigms are still correct?

Have we clearly defined the new process?

Have we identified the implications that these differences will bring?

_____

_____

_____

_____

# Step 6 – Define the revised model

So now you have compared the external Best Practice model to your current approach and identified the main differences along with those aspects of the current system that you want to retain.

What you must now do is combine the new and the existing to produce a revised cohesive model. It is this revised model that will be implemented.

In some cases, this will be very simple because you may be entirely replacing the current approach with the new model without any amendments.

## Building the processes

In most cases though, you will need to take time to work through the processes to ensure that you have blended the two approaches. The most likely result is a revised model that in some cases retains much of the existing system and in other areas is predominantly the external model.

## Development team

The preferred approach is to appoint a small team to produce the revised model. Once again, I recommend the flow chart approach to summarize the process flow, the responsibilities, roles, tools and so on.

Thus the output will be a detailed summary of the model combining the old and the new.

As before, the model is presented to an internal team of practitioners to "sense check" it. Once we have agreed upon the new model and its constituent parts, the next step is to build the detail.

## *Step 6 – Define the revised model*

Ask yourself:

| Are we sure that the new model meets all the needs? |
| --- |
|  |

| Are we sure that we have incorporated and blended the required aspects of the old model along with the new? |
| --- |
|  |

| Have we considered the implication of changing to the revised model? |
| --- |
|  |

We have now reached a similar stage to the one we had in the process to develop Best Practice from within the organization. We have defined a model, gained agreement to the model and we are ready to build the model detail and implement it.

Consequently, the final four steps follow the same process as the final steps for the internal model process.

**Step 7 – Build the detail for the Best Practice model**
(See pages 117-121)

**Step 8 – Implement the Best Practice model**
(See pages 121-123)

**Step 9 – Measure the results**
(See pages 123-126)

**Step 10 – Revise the model in the light of new learning and experience**
(See pages 126-128)

# 6

# Developing Best Practice
# from Scratch

Occasionally there will be a need to develop the Best Practice model from first principles.

In my experience, there are generally four situations when this may occur:

## 1. Entering a new market

The new market may be a new channel or a new geographical sector. Either way the assumption is that the characteristics of the new market are so different from the current market that the current model will no longer apply or at the very least must be significantly altered.

In some cases this will be obvious. For example, some time ago I was working with an international food manufacturer that wanted to develop its business in Africa. Clearly the models that were used in the more developed markets were not applicable and it was necessary to develop a completely new model based on the local market characteristics and requirements.

In this case, the differences were so clear that everyone accepted the need for a completely new model. In some cases though, the management team fools itself into believing that the new market is all but identical to the current market and that the current model will be effective. For example, many American corporations have sought to develop business in Europe just as many European corporations have entered the U.S. market. The trap into which many have fallen is to assume that the new market is all but identical to the home market.

Where the language is common, the danger is further enhanced. There are numerous case histories of successful U.S. and U.K. companies failing in each other's markets because they assumed that the two markets were identical and that the model that had delivered success in one market would be equally successful in the new market.

## 2. A market that has undergone significant change

Every so often a market goes through a seismic shift. Often this is precipitated by the introduction of a new technology. As a result, the current methods and processes become redundant. There are numerous examples to illustrate this phenomenon. We could consider the changes brought about by the introduction of new technology to support communications. The fax machine reduced the need to send documents. The introduction of e-mail reduced the need to send a fax.

In a similar way the channels or routes to market may change while the product remains similar. For example, many people now use the Internet to do their shopping. One of the few successful web businesses is Amazon, which began life by offering books for sale on line. The customers are still buying books and the books themselves have not changed but now they are able to complete the transaction without leaving home. In turn this caused the traditional book retailers to revise their approach, if not rather belatedly.

## 3. The market has experienced a paradigm shift

A similar situation to the previous one but in this case it is not new technology that has created the change but rather the way people think about things and as a consequence the way in which they behave. I discussed the concept of the "paradigm" and the subsequent "paradigm shift," first introduced by Thomas Kuhn in his landmark book *The Structure of Scientific Revolutions,* in an earlier part of the text.

Kuhn discovered that people prefer tried and tested ways or "rules" of doing and seeing things to such an extent that they can ignore evidence that does not conform to their view of the world. He called these "rules" paradigms. The majority of people in a similar situation are likely to use the same set of paradigms. Rarely, according to Kuhn, does anyone from within the current environment seek to challenge the prevailing views. The likelihood is that fresh ideas will come from outside the mainstream environment and will not be welcomed since they will challenge everything that the current order holds as true. The idea of a paradigm shift occurs when the evidence for the new way of thinking becomes overwhelming and everyone is forced to change or endure an adverse environment.

If we apply this logic to our current discussion, we can see that a management team is very likely to have its own series of paradigms. After all, that is exactly what a Best Practice model is all about; having a series of processes that you believe offer the best chance of success. Once people get used to working with these processes, they become reluctant to change. In just the same way that people can be reluctant to accept a new Best Practice model, they are equally likely not to want to change it once it has become established.

Consequently, the really radical changes that might be classed as a paradigm shift tend to emerge from organizations that lie outside the mainstream. A good example is a company entering a market from a different geography or channel. Of course, the logic here is counter to the logic discussed earlier. Earlier I argued that simply importing a previously successful model into a new environment may not lead to success because the new environment is likely to have some significant differences. Now I am saying that from time to time bringing in a model from outside can work spectacularly well to the extent that the whole market is revolutionized. Once again examples abound. We could consider for example the rise of the discount airlines booking directly and exclusively through the Internet. Discount airlines are not new but in the past they have been cheap versions of the mainstream airlines. The new discounters have brought very different operational models to bear and as a consequence have had a major impact on the business of the traditional airlines, which have been forced to reduce prices.

Other good examples where bringing in an external model has caused a paradigm shift include U.S. fast food models and their derivations into coffee shops. The Starbucks on Michigan Avenue in Chicago is identical to the one on Oxford Street in London or the shopping mall in Dubai. Previously the idea was confined to quick service restaurants. No one had considered the potential for an international chain of coffee shops. In fact the founder of Starbucks found it very difficult to raise interest in the idea when he first presented it.

So the point is that we need to be aware of the opportunities and threats offered by shifts in attitudes and in the way we do things.

Some managers find this difficult to contend with. Should they seek to introduce a Best Practice system or not, and if they do will it not cause their organization to be less reactive to a paradigm shift?

Our answer is that you should have at any time processes and systems that you consider to be the best available; in other words the Best Practice model. At the same time however, you must recognize that markets change and that the speed of change is increasing all the time. It is argued by some commentators that the only competitive advantage will become the organization's ability to react to change. As a result you will certainly have to change your Best Practice model at some stage.

I always recommend that organizations adopt a process of regular review of their processes to ensure that they really are delivering Best Practice.

## 4. New management team from outside the industry

The fourth situation where we see organizations wanting to build a new Best Practice model from scratch is where a new management team arrives, almost always from outside the industry. The typical situation is where an organization appoints a new General Manager from outside, often in anticipation of radical change or with the view to impose major change. The new General Manager tends to bring in senior managers with whom he or she has worked in the past. Occasionally we will find a whole management team has been imported. The new management team will have certain general paradigms about the way business should be conducted and these paradigms may not be reflected in the organization. Yet the organization may well be quite different from the ones with which the new management team is familiar so it is not possible simply to import a previously used model. Consequently the new team will want to develop a brand new model, which has its foundations at least in the basic business approach with which the team is familiar and at the same time is adapted to the new situation faced by the organization.

## Case example – Developing a new model

As an example, a non-food consumer goods manufacturer was acquired by a U.S. based private equity firm. The private equity firm brought in a CEO from one of the major consumer packaged goods firms. This CEO had spent his entire professional life with the large consumer packaged goods firms and was horrified to discover that the target setting, business planning, measurement and reporting processes were far less formal in the new organization. On the other hand, the systems with which he was familiar could not be directly imported and so the new management team set about working with external support to build a new series of processes that were founded on the paradigms of cascading targets, detailed customer management, coordinated sales and marketing plans, integrated production and operations, measurement and regular review.

## Developing a Best Practice model from scratch

As before we have a 10-step process to implement a Best Practice model from first principles. Once again the process follows a similar pattern. As before we will need to ensure that we have clarity about exactly what we want to achieve. This time we will spend much more time considering how we can achieve the objective. We will want to identify and assess a number of different possibilities.

Step 1 remains identical and that is to define success. Again we need to identify exactly what it is that we want to achieve and how we will recognize it. As before, it is essential that everyone understands and accepts this before we move on. Step 2 identifies the Success Drivers. This makes sense because here we are developing the model from within except now we are not just basing it upon the things we are already doing but instead we are looking for a new process that will reflect our new situation. Therefore we will want to consider from first principles what is most likely to cause success to happen.

Step 3 is where we need to identify the various options open to us to achieve the Success Drivers and to conduct a simple cost/benefit analysis. In other words, to consider the most effective and efficient ways of achieving the Success Drivers within the market constraints. We may also question our original assumptions about the most important Success Drivers in the light of more information, thought and learning. Step 4 goes on to select the preferred solutions and Step 5 requires us to synthesize the new model followed by a "sense test" as we did earlier. The remaining steps are identical.

## Developing a Best Practice model from scratch

| Step 1 | Define Success |
|--------|----------------|
| Step 2 | Define the Success Drivers |
| Step 3 | Identify the potential solutions and their implications |
| Step 4 | Sketch out the new model and its elements |
| Step 5 | Conduct the sense test for the model |
| Step 6 | Synthesize the Best Practice model |
| Step 7 | Build the detail for the Best Practice model |
| Step 8 | Implement the model |
| Step 9 | Measure the results |
| Step 10 | Revise the model in the light of new learning and experience |

# Step 1 – Define success
# Step 2 – Define the Success Drivers

Steps 1 and 2 are very similar to the process for developing the model from inside the organization that we discussed earlier. The only difference now is that to some extent we will be considering the Success Drivers without the constraints of any pre-existing model. We will be looking for Success Drivers from first principles and I have found that the best way to start is to make no assumptions whatsoever. The management team should work through an exercise to consider what the Success Drivers might be and to devise ways of testing these assumptions.

# Step 3 – Identify the possible solutions and their implications

Now comes the real difference. In the previous processes, we were basing our new model on what currently existed and we were heavily guided by what we identified as working best for us.

In this case we have no such model because by definition the previous working processes have been rendered redundant by the massive change to our environment characterized by the paradigm shift or simply because we have entered a new market environment.

## The danger of previous experience
Consequently, we cannot use our previous experience to guide us. In fact, I have found that it can be quite dangerous to rely on previous experience. Somewhat paradoxically for many people, I have found that the managers who are best at developing the brand new model are those managers who are not familiar with the previous approach. The managers who are most familiar with the previous methods are most likely to resort to these apparently tried and tested ways. As a result, the "new" model tends to look surprisingly like the old model. The problem is that your environment is not the same and contains different influencers and you need a new set of rules whether these managers can see it or not.

This is why the development of a brand new model is most difficult; not because it is so hard to build a new model but because the people will always prefer the previous model and if we are not careful the new model will start to look surprisingly like the old model.

## Mix the development team

I have found that the best composition for the development team is to have a mix of managers. Ideally, a blend of the incumbent team who are familiar with the environment and a group that have little or no intimacy with the previous approach and who can genuinely approach the thinking without a previous history. Since we are likely to be discarding a certain amount of the previous approach, it is important to have people who can take an objective view and are not likely to defend previous processes simply because they had a hand in their development. The benefit of including those managers who do have familiarity with the existing model is that we are more likely to get total acceptance. If we rely on a team without any familiarity, then there is a strong chance that the new model will be rejected.

However, sometimes no amount of planning can prepare you for resistance.

## *Case example – resistance*

I conducted a project for a major pharmaceutical manufacturer. Part of the project involved considering new ways of launching new products. At an early stage, it was generally agreed that the company had too many similar products and that these products were confusing the customer, in this case the medical practitioner, and distracting the company's effort. It seemed to be a simple job to phase out some of these low volume products yet strong resistance came from the CEO to this plan. All manner of arguments were raised. It was only much later that someone pointed out that one of the products due for the axe was previously the mainstay of the business and it had been championed many years ago by a young product development manager who was now – guess who – the current CEO!

For most of us letting go is one of the most difficult of tasks.

## How do we achieve the objective?

So far we have defined our fundamental objective and those Success Drivers that we need to achieve. Now we want to explore different ways of achieving them.

The best way to do this is to attempt to forget about the daily issues and to consider the issue from first principles.

I usually find that the most effective way to explain this is through a real case study example.

## *Case example – first principles*

This company had been a dominant player for many years in a market that was largely static. Like many before them they failed to notice the subtle and then not so subtle changes going on around them. They had been losing share for some time primarily to competitors who had arrived from overseas markets. Initially these competitors were small and the company dismissed them as irrelevant or never even considered them as a threat. The new competitors used a different method to go to market. They recognized that the market was mature and static and that a significant number of the customers did not see value in the many support systems provided by the mainstream suppliers.

The new entrants offered a low level of service, had no sales or traditional marketing team and surprisingly inflexible customer management and delivery systems along with an automated order taking system. As a result their cost base was far lower and they could offer very much-reduced prices to the customers. The lack of service was compensated by the low price. The new entrants had a slow start but then as they became established and accepted, started to take increasing amounts of share.

To counter this, our company did more of what had originally brought it success. It offered greater services and put more money into customer support and service. The problem was that by now the customers did not need or value any of the traditional support and saw the traditional sales and marketing as a distraction. Our original company now found itself with a real problem in that its cost base had increased yet its share was continuing to decline.

However it was not until the market share had slipped below the level at which the production economies were being lost that a new CEO was brought in. It is always surprising how long organizations are prepared to cling to models that are obviously failing.

The new CEO was from outside this industry and recognized that the previously successful model was now driving the company to ruin.

One of the Success Drivers that was identified for this company during the early stages of the development process of the new model, was the need to have a certain market share. Without this share level, the economies of production would not work. The overseas new entrants had been prepared to take a loss for a period while they established themselves supported by their home business.

The implication was that the company would have to do business with a certain number of specific major customers since these were the ones that could guarantee large volume. This was the first major implication recognized during Step 3 of the process. Now this may seem obvious to us but the company had previously had no defined plan to win and secure large customers in preference to any others. In fact the sales force tended to concentrate on winning smaller and medium sized customers since they were easier to win and more manageable to serve. They were also, as we discovered through our analysis, the most likely to take their business elsewhere. The large customers were the ones who still valued the extra support provided by the traditional supplier. It was the smaller and medium sized customers who were less interested in the service and more likely to select based on price alone.

In order to win and secure business with the largest customers, the company had to make huge changes to its operation and its beliefs. It had to move away from its traditional production and operations focus to one that concentrated on the customer. The research and development team, for example, would have to work in tandem with the research team from a customer. The customer would be able to dictate quality standards and the company would have to be able to consider different requirements for different customers. The sales force and field support had none of the sophisticated processes and skills to manage large multi-site customers. Few of the sales team had the ability or interest to deal at this level. And so it went on.

## Clarify the basic issues

So the point here is that we need first of all to identify the most basic of issues; in this example what kind of customer should the company serve, in order to achieve its objective, and then go on to consider the implications. Very often the implications are profound and may require the company to question all of its previous assumptions and possibly make sweeping changes.

Clearly this Step will take some time because there will be analysis to be conducted and a wide range of different implications to be addressed depending upon the direction proposed.

It is important to spend the time over this Step since launching into an implementation without having understood the implications could be disastrous and likely to alienate everyone. Everyone needs to be clear on the objective and the plan. We should recognize that within the organization there are likely to be various degrees of acceptance of the new model. The traditionalists will not want change and will resist it while the "modernizers" will want instant transformation and may become frustrated.

It is also important to ensure that not only have you identified the implications for the achievement of the various Success Drivers but that everyone accepts them. Never forget that the new model will almost certainly ask people to work in a different way with different rules using different tools requiring new skills.

### Step 3 – Identify the possible solutions and their implications
Ask yourself:

Are we sure that we have questioned the traditional paradigms?

_____

_____

_____

_____

Are we sure that we have found alternative ways that could offer increased competitive advantage?

_____

_____

_____

## Step 4 – Sketch out the new model and its elements

You have now reached the stage where you have defined what you want to achieve and identified the things that will cause this to happen, that is, the Success Drivers. You have also considered a range of potential solutions and their implications that will lead you to achieve the Success Driver objectives. Within the consideration of the implications you will have paid particular attention to the needs and concerns that you are likely to encounter. In some cases, the implications will be significant yet may not be obvious.

Since this is such a critical area, I am going to offer another example from a case history.

## Case example – Common processes across markets

A common issue faced by many large corporations that are operating in a number of different markets is whether the corporation should be focused on the product groups or on the customer groups. Most companies have developed their business groups over time across different markets through organic growth and acquisition and there really has not been a need to consolidate them. The accepted theory was that excellence comes through focus on the specific needs of the product group and that it would not be sensible to mix very different product groups. This is the approach that the majority of firms have adopted and have structured themselves accordingly. The product group General Manager will be responsible for the profitability of the business unit in the country and will receive a bonus based upon the performance of the business unit. The General Manager will be primarily concerned about the performance of his or her business unit.

This is the model that has worked well for many years.

On the other hand, it is often found that large customers buy across the range of products and will therefore have trading relationships with many different people within the manufacturer.

More recently, the major customers of these corporations have been requiring that the corporation provides terms and conditions across the whole business rather than separate terms for each product group. Customers want to consolidate their purchases not only across a single market but in some cases across large regions, say all of Europe or Latin America, in order to have a greater buying power. They want common prices, terms and conditions and often will not accept that they must pay more for an item manufactured in Germany than for the similar item manufactured in Italy.

In response, a number of large suppliers have initiated major projects to consolidate operations and their pricing and terms across the region to focus on the customers. This in itself has been a significant undertaking and has caused all manner of concerns within the corporations.

When one of these corporations came to consider the implications of such a move they tended to focus, not surprisingly, on the external commercial issues of changing their relationship with their customers. They also recognized that they needed to create a central customer management function to negotiate with the customers rather than the old model of having lots of different relationships.

One of the issues that was not so well thought through was the impact upon the local product business unit General Manager.

The new model required the corporation to negotiate across all the products across the region to agree common prices, terms and conditions with the major customers who were operating in each market. Naturally these revised terms replaced those agreed by each of the local product group business units. In order to harmonize the pricing, some markets had their terms increased and others reduced. As a result, each product group found that the prices for its largest customers had been changed. This in turn had an impact on the profitability of the product group business unit. Although across the whole region the corporation was making more profit as a result of the regional agreement and efficiencies, some business units were making less profit and so the bonus for that General Manager was reduced through no fault of the General Manager. In addition, in the past, the local product group customer account managers had been seen as among the most important managers since they were responsible for the agreements with the largest customers. Now however with the new model, they had a very much reduced role which simply required them to police the new central agreement. Not surprisingly this caused great dissatisfaction at the local level.

### Think through the implications

So once again the point is that we should try to identify all of the implications and a good way to do this is to present the concept to an internal team of practitioners for comment. This is Step 5 and we will discuss it below.

Before we can do this we need to sketch out the model along with the elements that we anticipate. In essence this means having a summary of the new model and the way we see it working that is detailed enough to be presented and give people a reasonable idea of how it might work.

Many of the points raised earlier in the discussion about presenting the model apply equally well. The difference in this case is that we will not yet have the detail.

## *Step 4 – Sketch out the new model and its elements*
Ask yourself:

> Have we thought through all of the implications of the change?
>
> _____
>
> _____
>
> _____
>
> _____

> Are we clear how the change will impact the management team and the way in which they are measured?
>
> _____
>
> _____
>
> _____

> Are we sure that the changes will be supported internally?
>
> _____
>
> _____
>
> _____
>
> _____

# Step 5 – Conduct the sense test for the model

Steps 5 to 10 are almost identical to the Steps in the process for developing the Best Practice model from within the organization.

The difference is that Steps 5 and 6 have been reversed. In the model that was developed by studying internal Best Practice, we could be fairly confident about the model and conducted the Sense Test just to check the details. We felt confident to develop the details of the model before we presented it for final discussion.

Now we have a brand new model. I have found that it is more sensible to present the draft plans and processes to the "test" audience of practitioners at an earlier stage. The "test" group will be able to make further suggestions that will result in more significant changes.

We should also recognize the importance of carrying the top performers and the influencers with us so that when we launch the new model, there is more chance of it being accepted. People will be more supportive if they have had some involvement in the design and development. Of course you must be careful about who you pick to be in the "sense check" team. You want people who will see the need for change and will not be scared about radical and potentially threatening solutions. If you select the wrong people then you will either end up with a new model that looks curiously like the original model or you will be forced to make so many compromises that the fine horse we designed will be produced as a camel.

## Step 6 – Synthesize the Best Practice model

## Step 7 – Build the detail for the Best Practice model

## Step 8 – Implement the model

## Step 9 – Measure the results

## Step 10 – Revise the model in the light of new learning and experience

# Summary

We have considered three main routes to developing Best Practice processes in your organization. Each is similar in that it seeks to identify and implement a series of processes along with supporting tools and skills that will ensure that the organization has the best chance of achieving its stated objectives. The difference comes mainly in the source of the Best Practice raw material.

In the first case, we assume that the Best Practice model already exists internally in various pieces but that it needs to be identified formally and consolidated into one definitive process.

In the second approach, the assumption is that there is more to be learned from outside the organization. The second approach requires that we draw on work already done by others. The third approach assumes that we need to start from scratch in recognition or expectation of major change.

Whichever route is selected, one of the main issues is to ensure that people understand and accept the need for change. All too often initiatives concentrate on elegant intellectually pleasing solutions while forgetting that the plan will be implemented by real people with real needs and fears.

The sad reality is that too many Best Practice initiatives fail to deliver the promised benefits. We know this because it is confirmed every time an industry group conducts a survey.

In the final section, I will consider the most common reasons why the initiatives fail.

# 7

# Why Does It Go Wrong?

Every so often, an organization will conduct a survey to determine the success of new initiatives in corporations. The results tend to make depressing reading since they invariably show that the success rate is very low.

We have compiled the results of a series of studies done by different organizations over recent years to produce an amalgamated figure.

The amalgamated figure suggests that around three quarters of all change-related initiatives are deemed to have failed by the organization that implemented them.

This is a remarkable figure especially when we realize that around 80% of U.S. corporations claim to have embarked on a major change initiative over the last five years. Of course, not all of these initiatives are Best Practice initiatives but nevertheless the point remains that most of the time the effort is deemed to be unsuccessful.

A Best Practice initiative is clearly a change-related initiative. It is hard to see how any Best Practice implementation could occur without change of some sort. In some cases, the change will be significant as we ask people to do quite different things in different ways. It is important that we take our own medicine and learn the mistakes made by others ("worst practice" if you like) if we are to give ourselves the best chance of success.

Over the course of my work, I have been invited on a number of occasions to assess the progress of a Best Practice initiative or to identify the reasons why a previously developed Best Practice initiative is not producing the expected results. I have been able to compile a summary of the most likely reasons why the Best Practice initiatives tend to fail or at least are not as effective as they might be. The list is not in any particular order and the reasons are not mutually exclusive. Normally we will observe a number of problems with a failing initiative. One problem might be the cause of or might exacerbate another.

There are often many reasons cited for the failure of new initiatives. I find that they can be grouped into a number of common categories:

- lack of understanding and normal fear of change
- lack of management support and focus
- lack of tools, skills and knowledge of how to do things
- general negative or cynical attitude allowed to pervade the organization.

## Why does it go wrong? – top reasons

### 1. Failing to explain the reasons for the initiative

It has long been established that people are more likely to support something if they feel that they are part of it and less likely to support the same thing if they do not feel part of it.

Simply imposing processes and systems on people without adequate explanation is almost guaranteed to result in a problem with the implementation.

Now every manager knows this, or at least will claim to know it. So why, I often wonder, do we always find that one of the most common complaints expressed by the practitioners of a failing initiative is a lack of explanation and understanding. Even when the team does not actively complain, we can deduce a lack of understanding through a simple questionnaire to assess understanding.

If I have been responsible in some way for a solution, then I am far more likely to support and defend the solution than the person who has had no involvement and merely observes. Simply telling me to do something or asking me to change the way I am used to doing something, is not likely to have the desired effect.

The preferred option is to involve everyone in the development process to some extent. However, this is unlikely to be practical in many situations and so a compromise is required. I have found that taking the time to explain the reasons and rationale for a course of action and offering the opportunity for discussion and questions will go a long way to help people to feel that they are part of the solution.

I usually recommend the use of a review questionnaire at critical periods of the initiative. The questionnaire is short and simple and tests the current understanding and perception. It acts as an early warning system of potential problems further along the line and ensures that the company can resolve the issue before it becomes a problem. The most common issue that is revealed in these questionnaires is one of understanding. Not necessarily understanding the detail of the process but the reasons for the change in the first place. Most people will be perfectly satisfied with the status quo.

## 2. No common agreement about the Objective and/or the Success Drivers

Without this basic agreement all initiatives are doomed. No amount of enthusiasm or hard work can replace the need to have everyone working toward an agreed common goal. This it true of the most senior management team right down to the front line. And it is not just the overall objective that we need to define and agree. The Success Drivers must also be common. Without common Success Drivers we will find that different internal groups can use different and potentially conflicting measures.

## *Case study – conflicting Success Drivers*

A business-to-business manufacturer had sought to refocus its business and had supported this process with external consultants. The consultants had identified that there were few internal controls or measures and no sense of responsibility at local level. They had recommended that the company introduce measures and ensure that managers were held accountable. At the same time the company took steps to reduce costs across its entire organization. All this sounds reasonable.

Some time later the company was facing a catastrophic loss of business. A brief investigation revealed intense customer dissatisfaction. Complaints revolved around product quality, delivery and customer service.

An internal review showed that the production team was now measured on production efficiency, in other words the number of units produced per hour. The administration and order processing team was measured on the speed of processing an order. The logistics team was measured on the time and cost taken to get the product to the customer. The sales team was measured on sales volume. Each group was paid a monthly bonus directly linked to the achievement of the objective that was specific to that particular team.

As a consequence, the sales team promised the earth and discounted heavily to capture the order. Production made a lot of product that was not required and to a much lower quality than was acceptable to the customer. Logistics only wanted to ship when it was convenient for them. Sales processing was not interested in dealing with customer calls beyond placing the order. Everyone had a clear objective but these objectives were destroying the company.

## 3. Fear of change and the implications of change

Even if people have not had a poor experience in the past, many are likely to be concerned. The fear of change results from a fear of the unknown. We are asking people to move from a world where they know what to expect to one where they do not. We will find that some people are even reluctant to move away from a clearly bad situation, apparently preferring the situation that is known even if it is bad.

Once again the key is to anticipate and to provide clear and open communication throughout the process. I normally find that once people are clear about what will happen, their role, the implications and the timing then most will be reasonably comfortable. Of course we are assuming here that everyone trusts the senior management team.

So much has been written about change in organizations and some people make their careers out of advising about change. The key point is to ensure that you have considered how people are likely to respond and that you have considered their interests as their prime motivator.

## 4. Fear of short-term commercial loss

One of the common criticisms of modern business is that it is far too short term.

A company is required to report its earnings on a quarterly basis and the market may quickly dump the stock of any corporation that fails to hit its quarterly targets. The average manager is in position for a very short time before moving on. There is an expectation among many that individual success is associated with change of role.

Experience shows that even the most senior corporate managers are more concerned with the daily management and short-term issues of the business. It should come as no surprise therefore to find that many managers become very nervous and are reluctant to make changes that may directly or indirectly impact the short-term business trading, even though the argument for the change is seemingly clear.

For example, an often-encountered problem is the company with a product range that is far too large. Companies tend to be very keen to launch new products but very reluctant to withdraw them. Even when it can be shown that the cost of maintaining the product renders it uneconomic even before the issues concerning loss of focus are considered, some managers will still hang on. The oft-cited response is that if we lose the product then we will automatically lose the business accounted for by the product.

Here is a classic example to make the point.

### *Case history – Product profusion*

A manufacturer of confectionery had had a marketing policy of increasing sales of the core line by introducing different flavors and varieties. The company had dozens of different varieties of the same product and many managers saw this as a core strength. An internal audit revealed that many of the varieties were not profitable. A consumer survey showed that while people were happy to try new varieties, they inevitably retuned to the few favored ones. Worse, an external audit showed that the smaller retailers were often out of stock of the best selling varieties because they were carrying stocks of the less popular varieties and were reluctant to buy more product until the current stock had sold out. The company's response was to offer smaller packages to the retailer, which in turn were more expensive to produce.

At no point did any internal manager suggest that the best policy would be to radically reduce the product portfolio. It was not until the business had been bought by a larger international competitor that this action was taken. The marketing effort was focused on the few most popular varieties and as a result overall sales increased.

You need to ensure that you are putting aside at least some time to consider the medium term and the place you want to be in say two to three years.

## 5. Not winning the hearts and minds of the middle managers

The point of bottleneck for many initiatives is at the middle manager level. It was expressed by a manager in the following way

"The senior team see the benefits, the junior managers want to progress but for the guys in the middle its just a threat."

It is essential that everyone plays a part in the new initiative and feels that their best interests lie in ensuring that the initiative is a success. Without this all we will get is lip service and no change.

## 6. The new process is not sufficiently clear and detailed

An old management adage holds that there are only three reasons why people do not do something.

1. They do not know that it should be done.
2. They know it should be done but do not know how to do it.
3. They know it should be done and how to do it but do not want to do it.

This point deals with the second reason – people do not know how to do things.

You need to ensure that the action you expect is clear and that you provide the right environment in terms of tools, skills, follow up and support.

It is the follow up that is most useful in identifying these types of issues. Once again, simply sending everyone on a seminar will achieve little without the ongoing support and development processes in place.

My preference is to ensure that every manager is responsible for ensuring that his or her direct reports have all the tools and skills in addition to the understanding. In this way, the process starts with the most senior manager and continues throughout the organization to the very front line.

Any new process must be sufficiently detailed so that it can be implemented properly.

As a checklist, each person must be able to answer the following questions.

- What is my role?
- Why is it important?
- What must I actually do?
- How am I measured?
- When will my performance be appraised?
- What tools do I have?
- What skills must I use?
- To whom do I go for help?

This implies training and I have found many initiatives lose their effectiveness because insufficient attention is given to skills development.

Passing off the training responsibility to a third party or the HR department is not effective. My strong recommendation is that every manager is made responsible for the skills development of his or her team. In this way, you ensure clear accountability and focus. The external third party or HR department can provide support and training tools but the responsibility for the individual's skills development lies with the line manager. Managers who are not able to train their team are not effective managers.

## 7. Lack of real support and follow through from the senior management team

It is a truism that everyone will look to the senior management team for guidance. The degree of importance assigned to any initiative will depend upon the visible support from senior managers. The support has to be seen to be happening; just making bold statements is no substitute. A common problem with failing initiatives is a lack of effective support from the senior management team.

Too many managers see the launch of the initiative as being the final step in the process. In fact it is the first step of the implementation. The key to success lies in the degree of follow up provided by the line managers at every level.

We can often trace failure of an initiative directly to a lack of management follow up.

When we talk about follow up, we mean the active implementation of the new process on a day-to-day basis.

You need to make sure that the new process is seen as part of the "way we do things."

## 8. General negative or cynical attitude allowed to pervade the organization

My final category is a bit of a catchall to cover a generally negative culture or attitude that has been allowed to build up over a period of time throughout an organization or part of an organization.

The incumbent senior team seem either oblivious to the situation or unable or unwilling to do anything about it.

A new management team will quickly identify the significant operational problems and will want to resolve them. Often a new process is required and it makes sense to base this on an external model. The difficulty comes if the management team has not identified the negative culture as a problem in its own right.

My experience is that major and often radical change is the best route forward. We prefer to shake the whole organization up so that it is all but impossible to return to the "old" ways.

It is not uncommon to find that in some organizations people have developed a cynical view about the true intentions of a senior management team as a result of previous experiences. In these cases, when we look back in history, we find one or more previous initiatives that have been presented as good for all when they clearly only benefited a few. We are likely to find the liberal use of euphemisms so that terms such as "modernization" have really been used to mean job cuts.

As part of the normal routine, I always recommend that you get a sense of the prevailing view and recent history of changes so that these concerns can be handled early in the process.

# Summary

### The top ten Best Practice fundamentals

1. If Best Practice is to have any meaning, it cannot be a vague intangible concept.

2. If you do not know how to measure it then you probably do not have it.

3. Implementing the Best Practice process does not guarantee success – however it can be shown to increase the chance of success.

4. Best Practice is not vested in one company.

5. Success today does not guarantee success tomorrow.

6. Talking about Best Practice is not the same as doing it, just as thinking you have a Best Practice approach in place is very different from knowing you do.

7. Similarly, having a Best Practice mode is very different from using a Best Practice model.

8. The Best Practice model is not fixed but will change as circumstances change and as new learning is gained.

9. If everyone is doing it then it is no longer Best Practice – it is common practice! It is not Best Practice to make products that work that you can deliver on time.

10. The Best Practice Model cannot be introduced without adapting it to your circumstances. Your company has a history and a current approach. It is difficult to try to replace them.

# Close

Recently I was asked to meet a President and her senior team to discuss the possible approaches to implementing Best Practice models within the organization. At the start of the meeting, the President explained its purpose to the assembled managers. One of the senior managers responded by asking to be excused as he had pressing issues to attend to and his business unit had "done Best Practice last month."

## Today, many people are talking about Best Practice

- To some it is the latest in a long chain of management techniques to be used for a while until it is replaced by the next great solution.

- To others it is just a means of confirming that their current approach is the best one and that there is no need to change anything.

- To my mind the concept of Best Practice is simple. It requires that you ensure that all of the things you are doing at the moment are most likely to lead to the achievement of your objectives at the moment.

- It is not enough to assume that this is the case. Your have to be able to prove it.

So the closing question is:

## "Are you sure that everyone is doing the 'right' things at the moment?"

The reality is that Best Practice development does not proceed as one big step. It is not something that we can "do this month." It is an iterative process and proceeds via a series of manageable steps. Question everything you do – ask if there is a better way. Implement only as much as can be absorbed – learn and move on. In this way the organization will truly be operating at its Best.

# Good luck!

# Appendix

## Agent Based Modeling

■  Unilever, the Anglo-Dutch consumer goods multinational, was seeking to develop a Best Practice model to deploy equipment in one of its production facilities. The traditional method of using observations and analysis of the current and possible options was not working due to the complexities of the liquid manufacturing line. In this facility, the various machines, chemical mixers, storage tanks and packaging lines all have different constraints, including their ability to be connected to other equipment, capacities, requirement for maintenance and product switching. Further complexity was added as a result of varying customer demand. Traditional analytical tools were not robust enough to model this situation.

■  South West Airlines faced a problem in early 2000 with its cargo operation. Even though the average plane was utilizing only 7% of the cargo space, at some airports there was not enough capacity to manage all of the freight. Managers were seeking to resolve the problem by putting cargo on the first available plane flying in the right direction. This apparently logical solution compounded the problem.

In both cases, traditional analytical and modeling techniques proved unable to solve the problem. The traditional correlation and regression approach was unable to cope with the many different and interconnected variables. In both cases a model was built and a solution uncovered using Agent Based Modeling.

**Agent Based Modeling**, which was developed from work carried out at the Santa Fe Institute and was originally used to model insect colonies, has since been used to model all manner of commercial situations from production and logistics systems to the way in which consumers behave in a supermarket. The great advantage of the Agent Based Modeling approach is that it is able to reduce a highly complex environment to a series of relatively simple to understand rules.

I will use a simple example to illustrate the potential. For years, researchers have been trying to derive a model to simulate the way in which birds fly in flocks. A large number of birds all seem to work together without a leader to form a cohesive group. Traditional modeling techniques had produced very complicated solutions, which, despite or perhaps because of their complexity, failed to produce a usable simulation tool. When Agent Based Modeling was applied, it was discovered that the complexity of bird flocking can be reproduced using just three simple "rules."

The three rules, "separation" (steer to avoid crowding local flock-mates and hence avoid collisions), "velocity alignment" (fly in the same direction as flock-mates), and "cohesion" (steer to move toward the average position of local flock-mates, i.e., stick with the flock), when coded into artificial bird agents and simulated, resulted in very realistic flock movement (so much so that this approach is now used in movies to simulate birds, bats, ants and even people).

A "flock" is a robust phenomenon that persists as a characteristic observable group despite obstacles (trees, buildings), despite predators (attacking eagles), and despite randomness in the environment and in the initial conditions (air currents, etc.).

Why should this be helpful? Well it demonstrates that complex situations can be modeled using very simple "rules." If we return to our earlier example at South West Airlines cargo distribution network, Agent Based Modeling was used to understand and explain the existence of large bottlenecks in that system. The problem proved to be exactly an emergent phenomenon, with no simple localized "cause." Having identified the problem, it was found that a small rule change would (at no additional operating cost) reduce the daily workload by 20%, the night-time workload by 70% and resulted in more on-time deliveries. The suggested rule changes were implemented and proved a dramatic success.

There are many examples in which ABM has provided small

improvements, but one big benefit of ABM is that, by providing a completely new way of looking at problems, it can sometimes lead to enormous improvements.

## Conjoint Analysis

A common dilemma faced by every organization is to figure out where to best apply its limited resource. Having determined what the variables might be, the next task is to decide their relative importance. For example, let us assume that you are trying to decide how best to use your commercial budget. The objective is to win and retain more profitable customers. There are many different things that you could do and many different things that you could offer the potential and existing customer. Each one bears a cost and you need to use your budget effectively. Where Agent Based Modeling will seek to model the whole situation and to determine the so-called emergent properties, another approach will focus just on the relative importance of the identified "drivers."

Conjoint Analysis has shown itself to be a useful tool when you need to determine the relative importance of a whole range of variables. For example, if we assume that we want to decide how the customer views the relative importance of each of the elements in our customer offer, we can use this approach to answer the question. Conjoint analysis compares these issues to determine the relative perceived value of, for example, different produce attributes including price.

In essence the technique works by identifying the core factors or influencers, the number of different options available for each influencer and the degree of utility that is applied to each of the influencers. Taking this approach allows you to compare variables that would not otherwise be comparable. For instance, is it better to provide a 24 hour customer contact facility or to offer a daily order and delivery service.

Conjoint analysis is a well accepted and widely used method to gain an understanding of the relative importance of a series of variables as individual elements or in bundles.

**Further reading**
There are many discussions available and most standard texts on marketing or research will have a section on conjoint analysis.

## Personal coaching

There is good evidence to suggest that supporting a Best Practice implementation with short but regular personal coaching sessions tailored to the specific needs of the individual can go a long way to improving the chances of a successful program.

# Index

Breinigsville, PA USA
20 August 2010
243912BV00003B/5/P